For Jessica

Contents

Bulletproof
Ajax

Jeremy Keith

New
Riders

Bulletproof Ajax
Jeremy Keith

New Riders
1249 Eighth Street
Berkeley, CA 94710
510/524-2178
800/283-9444
510/524-2221 (fax)
Find us on the Web at: www.newriders.com
To report errors, please send a note to errata@peachpit.com
New Riders is an imprint of Peachpit, a division of Pearson Education

Editor: Wendy Sharp
Copy Editor: Jacqueline Aaron
Production Editor: Hilal Sala
Indexer: Ron Strauss
Compositor: David Van Ness
Cover design: Mimi Heft
Interior design: Charlene Will

Notice of Rights

Notice of Liability

Trademarks

ISBN 0-321-47266-7
9 8 7 6 5 4 3 2 1
Printed and bound in the United States of America

Introduction

This book has everything you need to get started with bullet-proof Ajax. You'll find solutions to the challenges Ajax poses, illustrated with working examples. More importantly, you'll find explanations for the concepts and answers to the questions surrounding Ajax. So don't think of this as a programming book—even though you'll find plenty of code within. Instead, think of this as a guidebook to help you chart the unknown territory of using Ajax.

Ajax is a tricky technology to pin down. Most of the tools we use to make Web sites can be divided into two categories: browser technologies such as HTML, Cascading Style Sheets, and JavaScript; and server-side technologies such as Apache, PHP, and MySQL. Ajax sits somewhere between the browser and the server. Ajax requires JavaScript, which is a client-side language, but it also involves communication with the server. So whose job is it anyway?

With the explosion of interest in Ajax, server-side programmers are migrating to the browser in droves. They bring many years of experience in software design and object-oriented programming with them, but they aren't necessarily prepared for the unique challenges of developing in the browser. Meanwhile, client-side developers dipping their toes into the waters of Ajax are confronted with a tsunami of new technologies to be mastered.

There are plenty of books out there aimed at server-side programmers who want to learn about Ajax. This isn't one of them. If you're a Java programmer accustomed to creating complex objects, put this book down and move on to the next book on the shelf.

If you're a front-end developer, this is the book for you. You're probably well-versed in Web Standards. I trust you're using semantic markup and CSS, perhaps even some rudimentary DOM Scripting. If so, read on.

The prospect of learning Ajax may seem intimidating. Don't worry: it's not as complicated as the hype suggests. As you'll see, the JavaScript code isn't very complex. The hard part is making sure your Ajax applications are bulletproof.

In August 2005, New Riders published a great book called *Bulletproof Web Design,* by Dan Cederholm. Dan's philosophy centers around flexibility. Using flexible design elements that adapt to the user's needs, Web sites continue to work beyond the typical browsing environment. I believe that the same philosophy can be applied to Ajax.

Far too many Ajax applications are built like a house of cards, dependent on just the right stack of technologies in the browser. Browsers that don't support the required technologies are locked out and their users are turned away. To avoid this, you need to create flexible applications using bullet-proof Ajax.

I've created a companion Web site (http://bulletproofajax.com/), where you can download and try all the examples used in this book (http://bulletproofajax.com/code/). If you'd like to keep track of the latest developments in JavaScript and Ajax, visit my DOM Scripting blog at http://domscripting.com/blog/.

Acknowledgements

Dan Cederholm let me rip off the term *bulletproof* and use it for the title of this book. I owe him my thanks and a nice bottle of Pinot Noir.

The entire book-writing process went smoothly thanks to the stewardship of Wendy Sharp. She's responsible for getting me to write this book in the first place. Her dedication is beyond impressive: she managed to get the book wrapped up while planning a move across the country.

Thanks to Jacqueline Aaron for her stellar copyediting work. She took my leaden words and made me sound far more articulate than I deserve. I thoroughly enjoyed our discussions of style, grammar, and punctuation.

Thanks to my good friend, colleague, and technical editor, Aaron Gustafson. Working with Aaron was, as always, an absolute pleasure. Not only is he a JavaScript wizard, he's also a supremely cool dude.

I'm greatly indebted to Joe Clark, James Edwards, Derek Featherstone, Bruce Lawson, and Gez Lemon, all of whom kindly agreed to read and comment on my chapter on Ajax and accessibility. Any remaining inaccuracies are entirely my own.

My colleagues at Clearleft, Andy Budd and Richard Rutter, have been very patient with me while I've been skiving off work writing this book. Thanks for your understanding, guys.

Much of the material for this book was road tested at workshops and presentations throughout 2006. Thanks to everyone who came along to hear me natter on about this stuff. South by Southwest in Austin, Texas; XTech in Amsterdam; @media and Barcamp in London; and Web Directions in Sydney were incredibly fruitful sources of ideas and discussions. Thanks to Hugh Forrest, Edd Dumbill, Patrick Griffiths, Ian Forrester, John Allsopp, Maxine Sherrin and everyone else who put so much effort into those wonderful events.

Most of all, thanks to my wife, Jessica Spengler, for all the encouragement and support she gave me while I was freaking out about writing. I love you.

What Is Ajax?

1

From Ancient Troy
to Modern Web Design

In Homer's *Iliad*, Ajax is the name of the son of Telamon. As a Greek warrior, he was famed for his strength and courage. He carried a big ax and an even bigger shield to help in his fight against the Trojans. He also had a very cool name.

The name Ajax is so cool that it was used more than once in *The Iliad*. As well as the Telamonian Ajax, an Ajax the Lesser also fought in the Trojan War. The name has been reused ever since.

Ajax is the name of a British battleship that took part in the Battle of the River Plate in World War II. It was also the name of a rocket ship in *Flash Gordon*. The name Ajax has been used for at least four models of car, two record labels, a Dutch football team, and an arcade game. When the Colgate-Palmolive Company needed a cool name for a range of household cleaners, they chose the name Ajax.

Ajax is one of those terms, like Excelsior or Excalibur, that can be relied upon to conjure up images of strength. Perhaps the presence of an *X*, in combination with a mythological origin, is enough to bestow coolness on a word.

In the buzzword-filled world of Web design, it was almost inevitable that the name *Ajax* would show up sooner or later.

THE BALLAD OF JESSE JAMES GARRETT

Jesse James Garrett is an information architect, author and founding partner of the San Francisco–based company Adaptive Path. In February 2005, he published an essay on the Adaptive Path Web site titled *Ajax: A New Approach to Web Applications* (http://adaptivepath.com/publications/essays/archives/000385.php).

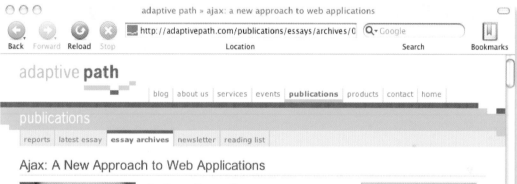

Figure 1.1 Jesse James Garrett on the Adaptive Path Web site.

In this essay, Garrett coined the term *Ajax* to describe techniques used by a new kind of Web application. Google Suggest and Google Maps were demonstrating that browser-based tools could offer the kind of interactivity and responsiveness normally associated with desktop applications. But there was thitherto no single word that could be applied to the technologies that made these applications sizzle.

When the seminal essay first appeared on the Adaptive Path Web site, the word *AJAX* was written using all uppercase letters. It was originally intended to be an acronym standing for "Asynchronous JavaScript and XML." While the first letters of these words map very neatly to the cool name of our favorite Trojan warrior, they aren't very effective in describing the technologies in question.

It's true that most of the new breed of Web applications are asynchronous. That is, interaction happens in the background without tying up the browser. But, as we will see later on, this isn't mandatory. It's quite easy to specify synchronous interaction.

The *X* for *XML* is particularly problematic. It implies that XML is a requirement for Ajax applications. This simply isn't true. To be fair, the letters *XML* also appear in the word XMLHttpRequest—the core technology used in most Ajax implementations—but XMLHttpRequest doesn't sound very cool.

Jesse James Garrett later updated his essay, making it clear that *Ajax* is not an acronym.

While *Ajax* may not work as an acronym, it's an excellent way of encapsulating a group of technologies in one word. That didn't stop some hardcore programmers from getting upset. "This is nothing new," they cried. "We've been doing this for years and calling it remote scripting. Ajax is just a buzzword."

While a geeky term like *remote scripting* was never going to sound as cool as a Trojan warrior, there was a kernel of truth to these petulant objections. None of the technologies used for Ajax are particularly new. Still, that's no reason to dismiss the term outright.

The word *Ajax* is a short, simple handle that describes a methodology which uses a cluster of technologies. It allows developers and clients alike to talk about important aspects of usability and design in modern Web applications.

But what does it mean?

Defining Ajax

Jesse James Garrett's newly coined term highlighted an explosion of activity among Web developers. A lot of companies and individuals had been separately exploring this new methodology. Now they had a word that they could use to describe their work.

Just three months after the publication of the original essay, Adaptive Path and O'Reilly Media organized an Ajax summit in San Francisco. Developers and designers got together to show what they were working on and describe how Ajax was changing the way they worked.

Following the summit, one of the attendees, Derek Powazek, described Ajax like this: "If the traditional Web was letter writing, Ajax is instant messaging" (http://www.powazek.com/2005/05/000520.html).

On traditional Web sites, the browser requests an entire page from the server. Then, the user clicks on a link or submits a form, at which point the browser sends a new request to the server. The server then sends another page.

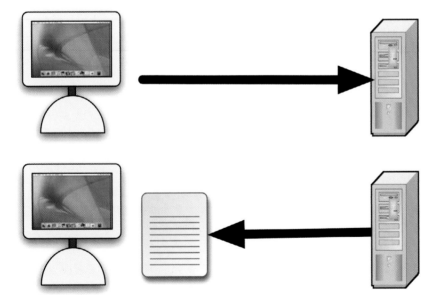

Figure 1.2 The traditional model of the Web. A client machine sends a request to the server. The server sends back an entire page. Rinse and repeat.

The Ajax methodology moves away from this page-based model. When the user interacts with a page (clicking a link, submitting a form, and so on), the server sends back a discrete piece of information. Rather than serving up an entire page, the currently loaded page is updated.

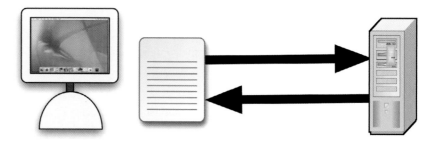

Figure 1.3 In the Ajax model, data is discretely transferred between the client and the server. The server no longer has to send entire pages.

For the user, this results in a more fluid experience. While traditional Web sites present users with a start-stop momentum, Ajax applications can offer faster and more responsive feedback—continuously.

THE BIG DEAL

This is my simplified definition of Ajax: a way of communicating with a Web server without refreshing the whole page.

This definition can provoke one of two responses. You could shrug your shoulders and say, "What's the big deal?" Alternatively, you could widen your eyes and exclaim, "That's amazing! It's a whole new paradigm for the Web!"

The truth about Ajax lies somewhere in between. It is an exciting technology. The ability to refresh just part of a Web page with information from a server can be used to great effect. On the other hand, Ajax is just a tool. By itself, it can't create a good user experience. Content is still king.

OPTIONS

According to my simple definition, many technologies would fall under the umbrella of Ajax.

Flash

Adobe Flash movies are now capable of communicating asynchronously with a Web server. That means you can update the contents of a Flash movie without a page refresh. That sounds like Ajax.

The Adobe Flex framework has given developers even more power. Flash is now a viable technology for delivering rich, responsive Web applications. (Detailing how to build Flash applications would take up an entire book. I'll leave that to someone else.)

Java applets

Java applets are little programs written in Java, not to be confused with JavaScript. Much like Flash movies, these programs can be embedded in Web pages. They are also capable of communicating with the server even after they have loaded.

The speed and responsiveness of the applets varies enormously depending on the specifications of the end user's machine. Java applets have never really taken off.

Frames

Remember frames? They aren't used very much these days, mostly because they're a usability nightmare.

If you build a Web page using a frameset, you can update just one frame without updating every frame in the page. Technically, according to my definition, that's Ajax.

My tongue is firmly in cheek. I'm not seriously suggesting that using frames equates to building an Ajax application, but there are a lot of similarities. As we'll see later on, many of the usability problems caused by frames are resurfacing in Ajax applications: problems with bookmarking and unexpected behavior from the browser's back button, for instance.

Hidden iframe

Using an inline frame, or iframe, is a step up from a frameset. An iframe can also be used as a secret conduit to a Web server. If a Web page contains a tiny, practically invisible iframe, its source can be constantly updated. Using JavaScript, the parent page can gather information from the updated iframe.

Google Maps uses a hidden iframe to communicate with the server. It's a clever solution, although it does feel slightly hackish.

XMLHttpRequest

The XMLHttpRequest object is an extension to JavaScript that allows Web pages to communicate with a server. It's perfect for creating Ajax applications. Jesse James Garrett had XMLHttpRequest in mind when he coined the term *Ajax*.

The biggest problem with XMLHttpRequest is how long it takes to say it. Even though there is an *X* in it, it was never going to catch on as a buzzword. The word *Ajax* is a lot shorter and snappier, and it's usually synonymous with using the XMLHttpRequest object. That's the kind of Ajax we'll be dealing with in this book.

The Ajax Toolkit

The XMLHttpRequest object is the engine that drives Ajax, but it doesn't exist in a vacuum. As Jesse James Garrett said in his original essay, "Ajax isn't a technology. It's really several technologies, each flourishing in its own right, coming together in powerful new ways."

ANY SERVER-SIDE LANGUAGE

Chances are, you want your application to respond intelligently to a visitor's input. The server needs to be able to make decisions about what specific information needs to be sent to the browser. In order to do that, you need to use some kind of programming language on the server.

There are countless server-side languages to choose from: PHP, Java, Ruby, Python, Perl, and many, many more. None of these languages is more suited or less suited to Ajax than any other. On the server, Ajax is language agnostic. Use whatever is most comfortable for you or your programming team.

XML?

You'd be forgiven for thinking that XML was a crucial component of Ajax applications. The term `XMLHttpRequest` itself, as well as its long-windedness, is somewhat misleading.

XML, which stands for eXtensible Markup Language, is a format for describing data. Ajax applications require some kind of structured format to deliver information from the server to the client. But XML is just one option. As we'll see later on, there are other ways of structuring data that are equally viable for Ajax.

Valid markup

It's entirely possible to build an Ajax application without using XML. But there is another kind of markup language that is fundamental to any Web site, with or without Ajax.

HyperText Markup Language (HTML) is the lingua franca of the World Wide Web. It is used to give semantic structure to content on the Web. After the content itself, markup is the most important and valuable tool for creating Web pages.

There is a disturbing trend among "serious" programmers to treat markup as a low-level technology that should be abstracted away from the developer. I couldn't disagree more. It doesn't matter how clever or fast the server-side programming is if the results are served up in carelessly generated markup.

Well-formed markup is a requirement if you want to manipulate a document on the client side (which is precisely what Ajax does). If the document isn't well formed, processing the document becomes unnecessarily complex and unpredictable.

Markup is well formed when its elements are correctly nested. Tags must be closed in the reverse order in which they were opened. For instance, this markup is not well formed:

```
<p>I told you to <strong>validate!</p></strong>
```

The closing </p> tag appears before the closing </strong> tag. But the opening <strong> tag appears after the opening <p> tag. This is the order in which the closing tags should appear:

```
<p>I told you to <strong>validate!</strong></p>
```

The strong element is now correctly nested within the p element.

The simplest way to ensure that your markup is well formed is to make sure that it is valid. The best tool for checking your markup's validity is from the World Wide Web Consortium (W3C) (http://validator.w3.org/).

A markup document is deemed valid if it correctly adheres to the guidelines specified by the W3C. You can specify exactly which specification you are using by including a Document Type Declaration, or doctype, at the top of your document.

There are a number of different specifications that you can validate against. These come in two different dialects: HTML and eXtensible HyperText Markup Language, or XHTML.

HTML allows you to be more lax. Some elements don't require closing tags, and you can write the tags in uppercase or lowercase.

XHTML is simply HTML reformulated as XML. That means it's a bit stricter. All tags must be written in lowercase, and every element must be closed. For stand-alone elements like line breaks and images, this is accomplished with a closing slash at the end of the element: <br />, <img />.

It is completely up to you whether to use HTML or XHTML to mark up your pages. Some zealots have argued that XHTML should only be served up with an XML MIME type. However, because some browsers can't handle that MIME type, they have also concluded that XHTML should be avoided completely.

Personally, I like the strictness of XHTML. The fact that all elements must be closed ensures that the documents will be easier to process. Of course, there's nothing to stop me from closing every element in HTML either. But by using an XHTML doctype, the validator is more likely to catch inadvertent errors in my markup.

Cascading Style Sheets

HTML and XHTML are excellent for describing exactly what your content is. They allow you to say, "This is a paragraph," or "This is a headline." But they don't (or shouldn't) describe how the content is presented. The technology for accomplishing that is Cascading Style Sheets, or CSS.

Using CSS selectors, you can choose which elements in your document you wish to style. Using the element selector, you can style all occurrences of an element. The ID selector lets you target a uniquely identified element in the document. The `class` selector finds all the elements marked up with a specific `class`. All of these selectors can be combined with one another to allow for fine-tuned presentational control.

Once elements have been selected, they can be styled using declarations. These declarations let you specify font size, color, and positioning.

Styles are usually declared in an external style-sheet file (or files), which is then linked to from the head element in the markup document.

As well as updating the contents of a document in a browser, most Ajax applications also update styles. In order to update the structure or the presentation of a document, you need a client-side programming language that can interface with the browser, the document, and its styles. That language is JavaScript.

DOM Scripting

Most Web designers are familiar with CSS, HTML, and XHTML. These W3C-approved technologies have come to be known as Web Standards. But there are other standards that aren't quite as popular.

In the same way that CSS can be used to specify the presentation of a document, a combination of JavaScript and the Document Object Model, or the DOM, can be used to specify the behavior of elements in a document.

The DOM is a standard that describes the structure of a document. In the past, competing Web browsers implemented their own proprietary models. The practice of controlling the behavior of a document was called Dynamic HTML, or DHTML—a confusing term because it sounds like another flavor of HTML. These days, the term *DOM Scripting* is used to describe standards-based behavioral control. DOM Scripting is integral to Ajax.

Summary

In this chapter, I've explored the history of the term *Ajax* and attempted to define what it means. In some ways, it's easier to explain what Ajax isn't:

- Ajax is not a specific technology.

- Ajax is not an acronym.

Instead, Ajax is a methodology. It's a way of working with a set of ingredients to create a more usable, responsive experience on the Web. Some of those ingredients are based on the server, but the majority are browser-based technologies:

- HTML or XHTML

- CSS

- DOM Scripting

- `XMLHttpRequest`

The `XMLHttpRequest` object is the glue that binds the server to the browser. Before looking at this mysterious object in more detail, it's important to have a good grounding in the Web Standards upon which Ajax is built.

You're probably already quite familiar with markup and CSS. You may be less familiar with JavaScript and the Document Object Model. In the next chapter I'll give you a crash course in these two crucial parts of Ajax.

JavaScript and the Document Object Model

2

Back to the Basics

The most important technology in a Web designer's toolkit is HTML. Without a markup language, you can't give the content any structure. Once the markup structure is in place, it can be enhanced with other technologies, such as CSS and JavaScript.

This chapter will serve as a crash course in JavaScript, a technology that is essential for Ajax. If you are already well-versed in JavaScript, you can skip this chapter although you might still appreciate this reminder of syntax and terminology.

JavaScript

Whereas HTML is a markup language, JavaScript is a programming language. Instead of specifying structure, it performs logical operations and calculations.

There are plenty of programming languages out there. What makes JavaScript different is that it can be run from within a Web browser. JavaScript is also found in other environments. It can be used to script PDFs, for example. But it is JavaScript's standing as the predominant client-side programming language that makes it so useful for creating Ajax applications. On the Web, the browser acts as an interpreter, capable of executing instructions that are written in the JavaScript language.

Like CSS, JavaScript can be embedded in a Web page, often within the head element. The most efficient way to use JavaScript, as with CSS, is to keep it in external files. These files can then be referenced by a Web page using `<script>` tags in the document's head:

```
<script type="text/javascript" src="/path/to/file.js">
</script>
```

JavaScript is usually written procedurally. That means you specify what you want to have happen in the order in which you want it to happen. The result is a script, much like a script for a play or a movie.

STATEMENTS

A single JavaScript instruction is called a *statement*. A sequence of statements is a *script*. A statement should always end with a semicolon:

```
statement one; statement two;
```

If a statement doesn't end with a semicolon, but it does end with a line break, JavaScript inserts a semicolon. It treats the statement as if it ended with a semicolon:

```
statement one
statement two
```

This can lead to some sloppy programming habits. It's best to always finish a statement with a semicolon, even if the statement ends with a line break:

```
statement one;
statement two;
```

Comments

Most statements in JavaScript can be read by machines. In order for a statement to be successfully executed, it must be written in the syntax of the programming language.

A *comment* is a special kind of statement that is intended for humans rather than machines. A comment is a statement that is ignored by the machine interpreting the script, but provides valuable information to people reading the script. Comments can act as useful reminders for the programmer, and explain more clearly what the script is trying to accomplish.

There are a number of ways to specify comments in JavaScript. If you want to write a comment on a single line, you can simply preface that line with two slashes:

```
// this is a comment
```

Because the JavaScript interpreter won't execute this statement, there is no need to add a semicolon at the end.

If you want to group a number of lines together as a comment block, you can open the block with a slash followed by an asterisk, and close the block with an asterisk followed by a slash:

```
/* This comment block
spans more than one line */
```

Documenting your code with comments makes life easier for yourself in the future. If you ever need to return to a script that you wrote a long time ago, any comments in the script help remind you of its purpose. Comments are also very helpful if you work as part of a team and other people need to understand your code.

At the same time, it's important to remember that every comment adds a little extra to the page weight and download time. Don't go overboard with comments. You will need to use your judgment in determining whether some code is self-explanatory or whether it requires explanation.

VARIABLES

Variables are the building blocks of any script. A variable is a label that refers to a value. Even if a value changes, its label stays the same. That makes variables very useful for storing, manipulating, and retrieving data.

Creating a variable is called *declaration*. In JavaScript, you declare a variable using the `var` keyword:

```
var variablename;
```

Variable names can be made up of letters, numbers (although they can't begin with numbers), underscores, and some other characters. Spaces are not allowed in variable names. To get around this, you can use an underline to make variable names more readable:

```
var variable_name;
```

You can't use a hyphen, though; it is interpreted as a minus sign.

Another aid to readability in naming variables is *camelCasing*. The way I've written the word there is a self-describing example. Using an isolated upper-case letter in an otherwise lowercase name helps differentiate between words:

```
var variableName;
```

Variable names are case sensitive, so all of these examples would represent different variables:

```
var variablename;
var VARIABLENAME;
var variableNAME;
var Variablename;
```

JavaScript has a number of reserved words that can't be used as variable names. Most of these are keywords that are used by the language itself: `if`, `else`, `for`, `while`, `var`, and so on.

DATA TYPES

When a variable is first declared, its value is `null`. It contains no data. Providing a value for a variable is called *assignment*. You can assign a value to a variable using the equals sign. The value of a variable can be a string, a number, a Boolean value, or an array. These are called *data types*.

Some programming languages demand that when you declare a variable, you must also state what data type it will hold. In those languages, you cannot change your mind later on. If you specified that a variable will contain a string, you can't use it to contain a number. This is called *strong typing*.

JavaScript is a weakly typed language. You don't have to specify what kind of value your variable will contain. You can also change the data type of a variable at any stage.

Strings

A *string* is a collection of characters. There are no forbidden characters in strings. A string can contain letters, numbers, spaces, and any other characters.

A string must be enclosed in quotation marks. You can use either single or double quote marks, but you must be consistent within each string. If you open a string with a single quote mark, it must close with a single quote mark:

```
var name;
name = 'Jeremy Keith';
```

You can declare a variable and assign its value in one statement:

```
var name = 'Jeremy Keith';
```

Multiple declarations and assignments can also be combined into one var statement by using commas to separate variables:

```
var first_name = 'Jeremy', last_name = 'Keith';
```

Because quotation marks are used to indicate the start and the end of a string, you would think they were forbidden characters within a string. In fact, you can use them within a string, but you need to explicitly state that they should be treated as part of the string itself. This is called *escaping*. In JavaScript, the backslash is used to escape characters:

```
var remark = 'That\'s my name';
```

In this case, the problem can be avoided by using double quote marks:

```
var remark = "That's my name";
```

But if you use double quote marks to contain a string, any double quote marks within the string need to be escaped with a backslash. These two statements are functionally identical:

```
var remark = "He is 5'10\" tall";
var remark = 'He is 5\'10" tall';
```

It's completely up to you whether you want to use single or double quote marks. For consistency's sake, it's best to choose one or the other and stick to it for the entire script instead of switching back and forth between the two.

Numbers

If you want a variable to contain a number, you don't need to enclose the value in single quotes, double quotes, or anything else. You can simply assign the number to the variable:

```
var year = 2006;
```

Numbers don't have to be positive. You can use negative numbers:

```
var score = -50;
```

You aren't limited to whole numbers either:

```
var average = 7.59;
```

Boolean values

While there are an infinite number of possible values for strings and numbers, there are only two possible values for a variable that contains a Boolean value. It is either true or false:

```
var happy = true;
var rich = false;
```

Boolean values aren't contained within quotes. If I used quotes around the word *true,* it would be a string.

Boolean values might seem very limited, but they underpin everything in a programming language. Boolean logic is the driving force in every computer. The flow of an electric current in a circuit is either on or off. It is either true or false. This is why binary is the universal language of computing. One is true. Zero is false.

As well as values for true and false, JavaScript has concepts of "truthiness" and "falsiness."

If a variable has been declared but hasn't yet been explicitly assigned a value, its default value, null, is a "falsey" value. It doesn't have an explicit value of false but testing the variable name will return false because null is "falsey."

Once a variable has been assigned any value at all, it is "truthy." This is very useful if you need to test for the existence of a variable with any kind of value. If the variable name evaluates to true, it exists and it has a value. If the variable name evaluates to false, either it has never been declared, or no value has been assigned to it.

Be careful, though. The number zero is a falsey value. So even if you explicitly state that a variable has a value of zero, a simple Boolean comparison will return false.

You can use one and zero as alternatives to `true` and `false`:

```
var happy = 1;
var rich = 0;
```

Arrays

All of the data types you've seen so far are called *scalars*. If a variable is a scalar, it can hold a single value. There is another data type called an *array*. Unlike a scalar, an array can hold multiple values within one variable. The values held within an array are called *members*.

You can declare an array using the new keyword:

```
var fruit = new Array();
```

Or you can use brackets as shorthand:

```
var fruit = [];
```

In an array you can combine declaration and assignment in one statement, just as you can in a scalar. To assign members to an array, separate each one with a comma:

```
var fruit = ["apple", "orange", "banana"];
```

The members of an array can be strings, numbers, Boolean values, or other variables. You can mix data types within an array:

```
var details = ["Jeremy Keith", 35, true];
```

Because an array itself is a kind of variable, you can store arrays within arrays:

```
var fruit = ["apple", "orange", "banana"];
var meat = ["beef", "chicken", "lamb"];
var food = [fruit, meat];
```

When you combine declaration and assignment of an array, each member is automatically given an *index*. An index is a number that denotes the member's position in the array. If you assign members after declaring an array, you will need to provide an index for each member:

```
var fruit = [];
fruit[0] = "apple";
fruit[1] = "orange";
fruit[2] = "banana";
```

Notice that the index begins at zero. Unlike human beings, most programming languages begin counting from zero instead of one.

To find out how many members are in an array, you can query the array's length. This alert statement pops up a dialog with the length of the fruit array:

```
alert ( fruit.length );
```

This gives a result of 3.

Wait a minute... aren't we supposed to be counting from zero?

This is one of the confusing things about arrays. Although indices are assigned beginning with zero, the length is calculated beginning with one. So the length of an array will always be one more than the array's last index.

The fruit array has three members. Its length is 3. The first member is fruit[0], the second member is fruit[1], and the third member is fruit[2]. There is no fruit[3], even though the length of the array is 3.

There is another kind of array, called an *associative array,* or *hash*. In an associative array, strings are used for the indices instead of numbers:

```
var details = [];
details["name"] = "Jeremy Keith";
details["age"] = 35
details["married"] = true;
```

The value of a member can then be retrieved using the index string:

```
alert ( details["age"] );
```

This returns the value 35.

OPERATORS

Storing values in variables is handy, but a programming language needs to do more than that. In order for JavaScript to fulfill your goal, it needs to perform the tasks you set it. The simplest kinds of tasks are called *operations*.

Arithmetic

Adding two numbers together is an operation. Subtracting one number from another number is also an operation. These examples, as well as multiplication and division, are *mathematical operations*.

Each mathematical operation has a corresponding *operator*. The operator is the symbol that indicates what kind of operation should be performed. For addition, the operator is the plus sign. For subtraction, it's the minus sign. The operator for multiplication is the asterisk, and for division it's the slash.

```
var addition = 5 + 3;
var subtraction = 15 - 7;
var multiplication = 4 * 2;
var division = 24 / 3;
```

Most useful of all, you can carry out operations on variables:

```
var year = 2006;
var age = 35;
var birth = year - age;
```

Some operations can be specified in shorthand. To decrement a number by one, use two subtraction operators together:

```
var price = 10;
price--;
```

The value of `price` is now 9. This is equivalent to writing the following:

```
price = price - 1;
```

To increment a value by one, use two plus signs together:

```
var year = 2006;
year++;
```

The operator for addition, the plus sign, serves a dual role. As well as adding up numbers, it can join strings together:

```
var adjective = "bullet" + "proof";
```

The variable adjective now contains the string "bulletproof" as its value.

Joining strings together like this is called *concatenation*. As well as concatenating strings, you can concatenate a string with a number. The number is automatically converted to a string, so the result is always a string:

```
var letters = "thx";
var numbers = 1138;
var result = letters + numbers;
```

The variable result contains the value "thx1138".

Comparison

Not all operations are mathematical. Sometimes you will want to compare one value with another. *Comparison operators* allow you to do this.

Using a comparison operator, you can find out if one value is greater than another, or if one value is less then another, or if two values are the same. This is accomplished with the symbols for greater than (>), less than (<), or two equals signs together (==). Remember, a single equals sign is used for assignment, not comparison.

if

The result of a comparison is always a Boolean value, true or false. A comparison needs to be contained in a conditional control structure. The most common control structure is the if statement.

```
if ( x < y ) {
// do something
}
```

After the if keyword, a comparison is written in parentheses. If the result of the comparison is true, then everything in the curly braces will be executed.

```
if ( x == y ) {
   alert ( x+" has the same value as "+y );
}
```

You can extend the `if` statement with an `else` clause. If the comparison in the `if` statement evaluates to false, then whatever follows the `else` clause will be executed:

```
if ( x > y ) {
   alert ( x+" is greater than "+y );
} else {
   alert ( x+" is not greater than "+y );
}
```

As well as the more straightforward comparison operators, you can also use these compound operators: >= means greater than or equal to, and <= means less than or equal to.

If you want to find out if two values are not equal, you can negate the equality operator using an exclamation mark; != is the opposite of ==.

```
if ( x != y ) {
   alert( x+" is not equal to "+y );
}
```

Equality and identity

The equality and inequality operators check for truthiness and falsiness. If two values are falsey, an equality comparison will return true.

If that sounded like complete gobbledygook, maybe this example will make it clearer:

```
var x = false;
var y = 0;
if ( x == y ) {
   alert ( x+" is equal to "+y );
}
```

The variable x has a value of `false`. The variable y has a value of 0 (zero). Zero is another way of saying false, so the comparison evaluates to true.

To find out whether values are not just equal, but also identical, use the identity operator, which is three equals signs (===).

To recap, the equals sign has different meanings depending on how many of them are used:

- Use = for assignment.

- Use == to find out if two values are equal.

- Use === to find out if two values are identical.

The operator for "not identical to" is !==.

```
var x = false;
var y = 0;
if ( x !== y ) {
  alert( x+" is not identical to "+y );
}
```

Logic

Using an exclamation point to negate a comparison is an example of a logical operation. The exclamation point is the *not* operator. There are two other logical operators, *or* and *and*.

The *or* operator lets you widen the scope of a control structure, such as an if statement. When conditions are combined using the *or* operator, a result of true will be returned as long as any of the conditions are met. The *or* operator is represented by two vertical pipe symbols:

```
if ( x < y || x > y ) {
  alert ( x+" is less than or greater than "+y );
}
```

The *and* operator, represented by two ampersands (&&), narrows the scope of a control structure. When conditions are joined together with the *and* operator, all the conditions must be met in order for the control structure to return true:

```
if ( x < y && x > y ) {
  alert ( "This is impossible!" );
}
```

No matter how many conditions are joined together inside the parentheses, an if statement can only ever return either true or false.

LOOPS

The `if` statement is an example of a conditional control structure. Other control structures are used to execute the same piece of code over and over. These are called *loops*.

while

The `while` statement looks a lot like the `if` statement. The difference is that the statement or statements inside the curly braces will be executed as long as the condition evaluates to true:

```
while ( x < y ) {
// do something
}
```

It's important that something happens inside the curly braces to change the condition so that it eventually evaluates to false. Otherwise, the loop will carry on forever. Here, the `alert` statement will be looped five times:

```
var i = 0;
while ( i < 5 ) {
  alert ( x );
  x++;
}
```

If the test condition evaluates to false the very first time it is executed, the statement or statements inside the curly braces will never be executed:

```
var i = 5;
while ( i < 5 ) {
  alert ( "You will never see this message." );
}
```

do...while

The `do...while` control structure is very similar to the `while` loop. The difference is that the statement or statements inside the curly braces will be executed at least once:

```
var i = 5;
do {
  alert ( "You will see this message once." );
} while ( i < 5 );
```

The loop is executed once, and then the test condition is evaluated. If the test condition evaluates to true, the loop will be executed again:

```
var i = 0;
do {
   alert ( i );
   i++;
} while ( i < 5 );
```

for

In the loops I've shown so far, I began by initializing a variable before the loop. The loop itself has a test condition that uses the variable. Within the loop, the value of the variable is altered, ensuring that the loop won't execute forever.

In the for loop, these three statements—the initialization statement, the test condition, and the alteration statement—are all contained in parentheses and separated by semicolons:

```
for ( var i = 0 ; i < 5 ; i++ ) {
   alert ( i );
}
```

The for loop is especially useful for looping through all the elements in an array:

```
var fruit = ["apple", "orange", "banana"];
for ( var i = 0 ; i  < fruit.length ; i++ ) {
   alert ( fruit[i] );
}
```

In the initialization statement, I declare a variable called i and assign it a value of 0 (zero). The test condition compares this value to the length of the array. As long as i is less than the length of the array, the loop will be executed. Finally, the value of i is incremented by one. The loop executes three times: the length of the fruit array.

FUNCTIONS

A *function* is a self-contained block of statements. Functions are very good at holding reusable code.

You can declare a function by using the `function` keyword followed by the name of the function you want to create:

```
function myFunction() {
// do something
}
```

Later on, you can execute the function like this:

```
myFunction();
```

The parentheses are there to take *arguments*. Arguments are values that you can pass to a function. Within the function, they act just like variables.

When you create a function, you can specify how many arguments it takes in a comma-separated list. Here is an example of a function that takes two arguments:

```
function multiply(x,y) {
  var result = x * y;
  return result;
}
```

The `multiply` function takes the arguments x and y, and multiplies them together. As well as accepting values, this function is returning a value at the end using a `return` statement. A function doesn't have to return a value, but if it does, you can assign the result of a function to a variable:

```
var days_old = multiply (35, 365);
```

A function is actually a kind of variable. Suppose you have a function that you have declared like this:

```
function shout() {
  alert( "Hey!" );
}
```

You could use a `var` statement to achieve the same result:

```
var shout = function() {
  alert( "Hey!" );
};
```

Note that because this is one long assignment statement, it culminates with a semicolon. The function is still executed in the same way:

```
shout();
```

If you want to refer to a function without executing it, treat it like any other variable and don't include the parentheses:

```
var annoy = shout;
```

Now the variable annoy is a reference to the function shout. The variable annoy is effectively a synonym for shout and can be executed the same way:

```
annoy();
```

If you include the parentheses when you assign a function to a variable, JavaScript will assume that you want to assign the result of the function to the variable. Here, instead of assigning a reference to the function shout to the variable annoy, the shout function will be executed immediately:

```
var annoy = shout();
```

So you can't include the parentheses when you're storing a reference to a function, but what if you want to store a reference to a function with arguments?

Suppose I rewrote the shout function to take a single argument, message, which is a string that will be output in the alert statement:

```
function shout(message) {
   alert ( message );
}
```

Now I want the variable annoy to store a reference to that function with a specific value for the message argument. This won't work:

```
var annoy = shout( "Hey!" );
```

The shout function will be executed immediately instead of being stored for later use.

The solution is to wrap the shout function in an empty function:

```
var annoy = function() {
   shout( "Hey!" );
};
```

This is called an *anonymous function*. As you'll see later on, anonymous functions are very useful for assigning functions to event handlers.

Scope

If you declare a variable outside of a function, it is a *global variable.* That means it can be used anywhere, even inside functions.

A *local variable* is declared within a function. It can't be accessed outside the function in which it is declared.

At first glance, it may seem that global variables are more useful because they can be used everywhere. In practice, global variables cause more problems than they solve. It's very easy to accidentally change the value of a global variable in an unrelated function. Local variables are much easier to keep track of because they are confined to a function. Ideally, functions should be self-contained, so it makes sense to use local variables whenever possible.

When we talk about where variables can be used, we are discussing variable *scope.* Variables declared within functions have local scope. Variables declared outside functions have global scope.

If you look at the `multiply` function again, you'll see that the only variable in it, `result`, has been explicitly declared inside the function, so its scope is local:

```
function multiply(x,y) {
   var result = x * y;
   return result;
}
```

Suppose I hadn't used a `var` statement:

```
function multiply(x,y) {
   result = x * y;
   return result;
}
```

When a value is assigned to the variable `result`, JavaScript needs to figure out the scope of the variable. There is no explicit declaration of a variable by that name within the function, so JavaScript assumes its scope is global and creates a global variable called `result`.

This could lead to problems. Suppose I had previously declared a variable called `result` outside the function. I want to use it to store a value for later retrieval:

```
var result = 50;
```

Next, I use the `multiply` function:

```
var days_old = multiply(35,365);
alert ( days_old );
```

That will output 12775, which is correct. But now look what happens if I output the value of `result`:

```
alert ( result );
```

That will output 12775 instead of 50, which was the value I had stored in the variable. The value of `result` was overwritten in the `multiply` function because JavaScript assumed I was referring to the same variable.

This could have been avoided if I had used a local variable within the `multiply` function:

```
function multiply(x,y) {
  var result = x * y;
  return result;
}
var result = 50;
var days_old = multiply(35,365);
alert ( days_old );
alert ( result );
```

Now the value of `result` has not been overwritten, and the `alert` statement correctly outputs a value of 50. I was able to use the same variable name twice without clashing. The variable `result` inside the multiply function is a local variable. The variable `result` outside the function is a global variable. They share the same name but are different variables because they have different scopes.

As long as you use local variables inside functions, you won't have to worry about inadvertently overwriting an existing variable. If you remember to always use a `var` statement the first time you assign a value to a variable, everything should be OK.

OBJECTS

While a function is a self-contained collection of statements and local variables, an *object* is self-contained bundle of functions and variables. When functions and variables are bundled up in this way, they are called *methods* and *properties*.

A method is a function that belongs to an object. A method can take arguments, just like a function. To execute a method, it must be preceded by the name of the object to which it belongs, and a dot:

```
object.method();
```

A property is accessed using the same kind of dot notation:

```
object.property;
```

You've already seen this kind of notation in action. Every time you access the `length` of an array, you are referring to the `length` property of the `Array` object:

```
array.length;
```

So an array is an object. It turns out that objects are everywhere in JavaScript.

Native objects

Every time you create a string variable, you are actually creating an instance of a `String` object. There are numerous methods you can invoke on any string. The `toUpperCase` method, for example, returns the string in capital letters:

```
var message = "hey!";
alert ( message.toUpperCase() );
```

This outputs the string "HEY!"

Strings and arrays are examples of *native objects*. They are part of the core JavaScript language. JavaScript also provides a `Math` object and a `Date` object. All of these objects come with presupplied methods and properties that are very useful for carrying out common tasks. The `Math` object, for example, provides a `round` method that can be used to round off to the nearest whole number:

```
var num = 3.14
alert ( Math.round(num) );
```

This outputs the number 3.

User-defined objects

You aren't limited to the objects that JavaScript provides for you. You can create your own *user-defined objects*.

To begin with, create a new *class* of object. A class is a template from which objects are made. Classes are created just like functions.

```
var Car = function() {
};
```

Using the this keyword, you can create properties and methods for this class. The keyword this is shorthand for "the current object":

```
var Car = function() {
  this.wheels = 4;
  this.start = function() {
    alert( "Vroom!");
  };
};
```

The variable wheels is a property. The start function is a method.

To create a new object from the class Car, use the new keyword:

```
var mercedes = new Car();
```

You can invoke the start method like this:

```
mercedes.start();
```

The first statement creates a new instance of the Car class called mercedes. The second statement executes the start method of the object.

Similarly, you can use dot notation to access the wheels property:

```
alert ( mercedes.wheels );
```

Don't worry if all this object stuff isn't clear to you. Object-oriented programming can be a tricky subject to understand. I will deal with user-defined objects in more detail later.

Host objects

Whereas native objects are provided by the programming language, and user-defined objects are created by the programmer, *host objects* are provided by the environment in which JavaScript is running. The host objects provided for JavaScript running inside in a PDF viewer will be different from the host objects inside a Web browser.

The most basic host object a Web browser provides JavaScript is the window object. The properties of the window object provide information about the browser window, such as its size and position. The methods of the `window` object allow programmers to create and manipulate browser windows. These properties and methods are collectively known as the Browser Object Model. You can thank the BOM for those hideous pop-up windows that pollute the World Wide Web.

While the BOM lets you query and manipulate the browser window, it doesn't provide access to the document within that window. To manipulate the contents of a page in a Web browser, the browser provides a different host object: the `document` object.

The Document Object Model

Early browsers gave JavaScript limited access to some parts of the currently loaded document through host objects such as `forms` and `images`. Version 4 browsers allowed access to more elements. Sadly, the competing browsers implemented completely different models.

Suppose you had a `div` element with an ID of `example`:

```
<div id="example">
</div>
```

Netscape Navigator 4 allowed you to access that element in JavaScript using this syntax:

```
var mydiv = document.layers["example"];
```

Internet Explorer 4, meanwhile, insisted on this:

```
var mydiv = document.all["example"];
```

Both statements achieve the same result. In order to get code working across browsers, developers had to fork their code with `if` statements:

```
if (document.all) {
// do something for IE
} else if (document.layers) {
// do the same thing for NN
}
```

This situation was intolerable. Standardization was required and, thanks to the W3C, it was provided in the form of the Document Object Model, or the DOM.

GETTERS

The W3C DOM goes further than any of the proprietary models. It allows access to any part of a document, whether it's an element, a piece of text within an element, or an attribute of an element. It isn't limited to Web pages, either. Any DOM-capable language can use the same methods to parse any kind of markup document.

The DOM provides a number of methods for accessing the individual components of a document. These methods are called *getters*.

getElementById

To access the `"example"` `div` with the DOM, you can use the `getElement-ById` method of the `document` object:

```
var mydiv = document.getElementById("example");
```

This is similar to the ID selector in CSS:

```
#mydiv {
}
```

The syntax is different but the aim is the same: you are accessing a specific element in the document so that you can manipulate it. With CSS, you can provide style declarations that specify how the element should be presented. With the DOM and JavaScript, you can query and update properties of the element. This means it is possible to update the contents of a document even after it has been loaded into the browser window.

getElementsByTagName

The similarities between CSS and DOM Scripting don't stop with `getEle-mentById`. CSS uses the element selector to get all the elements in a document with a specific tag name. This is how CSS would fetch all the paragraph elements in a document:

```
p {
}
```

The DOM provides an equivalent method with `getElementsByTagName`:

```
var paragraphs = document.getElementsByTagName("p");
```

The variable `paragraphs` now contains a collection of all the p elements in the document. You can treat this collection much like an array. You can find out how many paragraphs are in the document through the `length` property:

```
alert ( paragraphs.length );
```

You can also cycle through all the paragraphs by using a `for` loop:

```
for ( var i=0; i < paragraphs.length; i++ ) {
// do something with paragraph[i]
}
```

CSS lets you combine selectors. You can select all the paragraph elements within an element with the ID `example`:

```
#example p {
}
```

You can also do this with the DOM:

```
document.getElementById("example").getElementsByTagName("p")
```

getAttribute

CSS lets you apply styles to elements. That's why all the selectors reference elements. The DOM allows you to go deeper: you can retrieve the value for an attribute.

Suppose you marked up a paragraph with a `title` attribute:

```
<p id="intro" title="introductory message">
</p>
```

Using the `getAttribute` method, you can retrieve the value of this attribute:

```
var introduction = document.getElementById("intro");
var title_text = introduction.getAttribute("title");
```

The variable `title_text` now contains the string `"introductory message"`.

NODES

When you use methods like `getElementById`, `getElementsByTagName`, or `getAttribute`, you are accessing *nodes* in the document. The term *node* is normally used to describe connecting points in a network. You can think of a Web page as a network of interconnected nodes.

There are three basic types of node that make up a document: *element nodes, text nodes,* and *attribute nodes.* Text nodes and attribute nodes contain the content of a Web page. Element nodes are the building blocks used to structure that content.

Every node in a document is contained in another node. This means that the network of interconnected nodes in a document has a very straightforward structure: it is a tree of nodes. More specifically, it resembles a family tree.

Take a look at this simple XHTML document:

```
<!DOCTYPE html PUBLIC "-//W3C//DTD XHTML 1.0 Strict//EN"
"http://www.w3.org/TR/xhtml1/DTD/xhtml1-strict.dtd">
<html>
  <head>
    <title>Simple page</title>
  </head>
  <body>
    <h1>Welcome</h1>
    <p id="intro">This is a very simple document.</p>
  </body>
</html>
```

Figure 2.1 A simple document as viewed in a browser.

If you view this document in a browser, you will see something like Figure 2.1. The node tree of this document is shown in Figure 2.2.

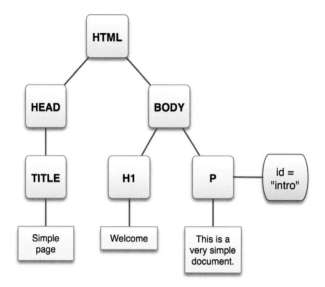

Figure 2.2 The node tree of a simple document.

The DOM uses the terminology of a family tree to describe the relationship between nodes. The html element is the parent of the head element and the body element. That means the head and body elements are siblings. The head element is the parent of the title element. That means the title element is a child of the head element.

These relationships can be accessed through DOM properties.

parentNode

The parentNode property of a node will return a reference to an element node. Only element nodes are capable of being parents.

```
var introduction = document.getElementById("intro");
var container = introduction.parentNode;
```

The variable container now contains a reference to the body element. If you were to access container.parentNode, you would get a reference to the html element. So, using the parentNode property, you can work your way right up through the node tree.

Every node in a document has a parentNode. Every piece of text must be contained within an element. Every attribute must belong to an element. Every element, apart from the html element, must be contained within another element node. Even the html element has a parentNode, namely the document object itself.

childNodes

The childNodes property of an element node will return a collection of nodes. You can loop through these nodes just as you can loop through the elements of an array. The childNodes property has a length property that provides the number of children an element contains. If an element has no children, the childNodes property will return an empty collection with a length of zero.

Only element nodes are capable of having children.

Note that some browsers calculate nodes differently than others. Some browsers treat line breaks and white space between elements as new text nodes, while others ignore them. This could lead to inconsistent results from browser to browser.

You can see this for yourself by testing this code in different browsers:

```
var introduction = getElementById("intro");
var container = introduction.parentNode;
var children = container.childNodes;
alert ( children.length );
```

More often than not, you'll be interested in getting the elements contained by a parent. In that case, the childNodes property is overkill because it also returns text nodes and attributes. Instead, use the getElementsByTagName method and pass it the wildcard character, which is an asterisk:

```
var all_elements = document.getElementsByTagName("*");
```

The variable all_elements now contains a collection of all the elements in the document. Most of the time, you won't use the wildcard character on the whole document. Instead, you will use getElementsByTagName("*") on a specific element.

```
var introduction = getElementById("intro");
var container = introduction.parentNode;
var elements = container.getElementsByTagName("*");
alert ( elements.length );
```

firstChild

The `firstChild` property of an element node returns a reference to the first node in the element's `childNodes` collection. It is a shorthand way of saying `childNodes[0]`.

lastChild

Similarly, the `lastChild` property returns a reference to the last node in an element's `childNodes` property.

previousSibling

If two nodes share the same parent, they are siblings. That means they both reside in the parent element's `childNodes` collection. The `previousSibling` property of a node returns a reference to the node that comes before it in the parent's `childNodes` property.

nextSibling

Like `previousSibling`, the `nextSibling` property returns a reference to a node that shares the same parent as the current node. Specifically, it provides a reference to the next node in the parent's `childNodes` property.

nodeValue

As you can see, it's possible to use DOM methods and properties to navigate all around a document from any starting point. But all of these methods and properties only return references to nodes. If you want to retrieve the content of a node, you need to use the `nodeValue` property.

Suppose I wanted to retrieve the text that's sitting inside the paragraph with the ID `intro`. I might be tempted to use the `nodeValue` property like this:

```
var introduction = document.getElementById("intro");
alert ( introduction.nodeValue );
```

But this produces a result of `null`. The `nodeValue` for any element node is `null`. What I actually want to get is the value of the text node contained within the element:

```
var introduction = document.getElementById("intro");
var text = introduction.firstChild;
alert ( text.nodeValue );
```

Similarly, if I wanted to get the value of the text within the h1 element, this is what I would do:

```
var headers = document.getElementsByTagName("h1");
var text = headers[0].firstChild;
alert ( text.nodeValue );
```

I start by getting all of the elements with the tag name "h1." In this case, there is only one h1 element, so I'm only interested in the first element in the collection. The `firstChild` property of this element is the text node I'm trying to get to. By accessing the `nodeValue` of that text node, I get the string of text I wanted.

I can do all of that in one statement, but it isn't as readable:

```
alert ( document.getElementsByTagName("h1")[0].firstChild.
nodeValue );
```

SETTERS

The ability to navigate the node tree of a document is useful, but the real power of the DOM is its ability to manipulate the node tree. DOM methods let you add and remove nodes from a document. These methods are the *setters*.

There are three methods for creating nodes. These methods correspond to the three types of node that make up a node tree: element nodes, text nodes, and attribute nodes.

createElement

The `createElement` method allows you to conjure up a new element node. It takes a single argument, which is the tag name of the element you want to create.

This creates a new paragraph element:

```
var para = document.createElement("p");
```

This newly created paragraph element doesn't appear in the document. It's floating around in JavaScript limbo, waiting to be inserted somewhere in the document.

createTextNode

The `createTextNode` method works just like the `createElement` method, except that, as you might expect, it creates a text node. The single argument it takes is a string of text:

```
var text = document.createTextNode("I made this!");
```

Again, this won't automatically appear in the document.

setAttribute

The `setAttribute` method is the corollary of `getAttribute`. It lets you specify a value for an attribute of an element. The method takes two arguments: the name of the attribute, and the value you want to set for the attribute.

This sets the `title` attribute of the paragraph element node referenced by the variable *para*:

```
para.setAttribute("title","generated content");
```

appendChild

The `appendChild` method allows you to insert one node into another node. In other words, you can specify that one node should be the child node of another.

This inserts a newly created text node into a newly-created paragraph element:

```
var para = document.createElement("p");
var text = document.createTextNode("I made this!");
para.appendChild(text);
```

`appendChild` is always a method of an element node. Remember, only element nodes can be parents.

This same method can be used to insert generated nodes into the document.

Going back to our simple document, suppose I wanted to update the node tree by adding a new paragraph before the closing </body> tag. This is the original markup:

```
<body>
  <h1>Welcome</h1>
  <p id="intro">This is a very simple document.</p>
</body>
```

Here's the generated content I want to insert:

```
var para = document.createElement("p");
var text = document.createTextNode("I made this!");
para.appendChild(text);
para.setAttribute("title","generated content");
```

That creates a chunk of markup, referenced by the variable para, which looks like this:

```
<p title="generated content">I made this!</p>
```

I want to make this paragraph element a child node of the body element.

The easiest way for me to get into the document is by accessing the element that has a unique ID:

```
var introduction = document.getElementById("intro");
```

Now I can create a reference to the body element because it's the parent of the element I've accessed:

```
var container = introduction.parentNode;
```

Finally, I append my generated content using appendChild:

```
container.appendChild(para);
```

This adds the para node to the childNodes collection of the body element. When a node is inserted into an element using appendChild, the inserted node becomes the lastChild of that element.

removeChild

The opposite of appendChild is removeChild. This method lets you remove a specified child node from an element.

This removes the text node that's inside the paragraph with the "intro" ID:

```
var introduction = document.getElementById("intro");
var text = introduction.firstChild;
introduction.removeChild(text);
```

Summary

The combination of JavaScript and the Document Object Model is very power-ful. In this chapter, I've covered the basics of the JavaScript language and I've shown you some of the most useful properties and methods of the DOM.

DOM Scripting can be used to achieve some very impressive results. The structure and content of a Web page can be updated, even after the docu-ment has loaded. But this isn't Ajax.

Ajax involves some communication with the server. Ajax and DOM Scripting are very closely linked: you can use DOM Scripting to update a document with information sent from the server via Ajax. In order to retrieve that infor-mation from the server, you need to go beyond the DOM.

In the next chapter, I will introduce you to a mysterious and powerful object called XMLHttpRequest.

XMLHttpRequest

3

The Object of the Game

The XMLHttpRequest object isn't part of the DOM. Until recently, it wasn't part of any W3C specification. The success of Ajax has spurred the World Wide Web Consortium into unusually swift action. You can now find a working draft of a specification for the XMLHttpRequest object on the W3C site (www.w3.org/TR/XMLHttpRequest/).

Origins

The idea for an object that can communicate between the client and the server originated with Microsoft. The developers of Microsoft's Web-based mail client, Web Access 2000, needed some way of asynchronously transferring information to and from the browser. The development team for Microsoft Internet Explorer scratched that itch. Internet Explorer 5.0 for Windows was the first Ajax-capable Web browser.

The first implementation of this object was called XMLHttp, and Microsoft made it available only as an ActiveX object. ActiveX is a proprietary Microsoft technology designed for embedding multimedia files in Web pages. In some ways it is a competitor to the Java applet. Both Java applets and ActiveX controls allow developers to embed powerful tools inside a document in a Web browser. This power could potentially be abused; the threat of malicious ActiveX controls has continuously shrouded the technology with security fears.

The developers behind the Mozilla project followed Microsoft's lead, but they implemented the XMLHttpRequest object natively. Mozilla 1.0 was released in 2002. The same code base forms the basis of Netscape Navigator since version 6, as well as the Mozilla Firefox browser. Apple's Safari has included support for XMLHttpRequest since version 1.2. The Opera browser has been Ajax capable since version 8. XMLHttpRequest is even supported in the mobile browser, Opera Mini.

All of these browsers implement XMLHttpRequest natively. That leaves only Internet Explorer versions 5 to 6 requiring ActiveX support. Microsoft has decided to abandon the ActiveX approach and Internet Explorer 7 implements the XMLHttpRequest object just as any other modern browser does.

It's worth remembering that just because a visitor to your site is using a browser that is technically Ajax capable, it doesn't necessarily mean that Ajax is an option. JavaScript can be switched off. In the case of Internet Explorer before version 7, even if JavaScript is switched on, ActiveX support might be disabled because of security concerns.

Create an Instance

Creating a new instance of an XMLHttpRequest object is quite straight-forward in most browsers:

```
var xhr = new XMLHttpRequest();
```

But it isn't that simple in Internet Explorer. You need to create a new instance of an ActiveX object:

```
var xhr = new ActiveXObject("Microsoft.XMLHTTP");
```

Other browsers will choke on that. Meanwhile, Internet Explorer will choke on the syntax for creating an instance of the native object. The solution is to test for the existence of the object before attempting to create an instance:

```
if (window.XMLHttpRequest) {
  var xhr = new XMLHttpRequest();
}
```

This is called object detection. Here's the object detection to test for the existence of ActiveX:

```
if (window.ActiveXObject) {
  var xhr = new ActiveXObject("Microsoft.XMLHTTP");
}
```

To save yourself from writing this every time you want to do some Ajax, you can wrap up the object detection in a reusable function:

```
function getHTTPObject() {
  var xhr = false;
  if (window.XMLHttpRequest) {
    xhr = new XMLHttpRequest();
  } else if (window.ActiveXObject) {
    xhr = new ActiveXObject("Microsoft.XMLHTTP");
  }
  return xhr;
}
```

The function, called getHTTPObject, begins by declaring a variable called xhr and assigning it a Boolean value of false. The plan is to change this value over the course of the function.

An if...else statement takes care of the object detection. First, test for the existence of the native XMLHttpRequest. If such an object exists, change the value of xhr to a new instance of the object. If not, test for the existence of ActiveXObject. If that exists, assign a new instance of Microsoft's XMLHTTP ActiveX object to xhr.

Finally, return the value of xhr at the end of the function. At this stage, there are three possible values that the variable could have:

- An instance of the native XMLHttpRequest object.

- An instance of an ActiveX object.

- A value of false.

You can use the function like this:

```
var request = getHTTPObject();
```

This assigns the result of the getHTTPObject function to the variable request. You can now treat this variable as an instance of a cross-browser XMLHttpRequest object.

It is still possible that the getHTTPObject function has returned a value of false, meaning that the browser executing the script does not have Ajax capabilities. If you explicitly check for this, you can make sure you won't be asking older browsers to execute code beyond their ability:

```
var request = getHTTPObject();
if (request) {
// do some Ajax
}
```

BULLETPROOF INSTANTIATION

The getHTTPObject function works fine most of the time. But it does contain an assumption. Just because a browser supports ActiveX doesn't necessarily mean that the specific ActiveX object for Ajax also exists.

This is the case with Internet Explorer 5 for Mac. As it stands, the getHTTPObject function throws an error in that browser.

One solution might be to look at the user-agent string of the browser and check its name and version number. This is called browser sniffing. It's a very bad idea. User-agent strings can be spoofed, and browser sniffing inevitably triggers false positives. Object detection is always preferable to browser sniffing.

In this particular case, you can use object detection to test only for the existence of ActiveX, not for a particular type of ActiveX object.

JavaScript has a useful control structure for situations like this called the
`try...catch` statement. Using this statement, you can attempt to execute
some code and, if it doesn't work, you can catch the error. The error won't be
displayed in the browser.

```javascript
if (window.ActiveXObject) {
  try {
    xhr = new ActiveXObject("Microsoft.XMLHTTP");
  } catch(e) {
    xhr = false;
  }
}
```

The `try` block contains the attempt to assign an instance of the ActiveX
object to the variable `xhr`. If that doesn't work, the `catch` block sets the
value to `false`.

The `try...catch` statement can be used to refine the `getHTTPObject` function even further. Later versions of Internet Explorer can use a newer ActiveX
object to handle Ajax. Using a series of `try...catch` statements, you can
attempt to use the newest version and, if that fails, fall back to the older way:

```javascript
if (window.ActiveXObject) {
  try {
    xhr = new ActiveXObject("Msxml2.XMLHTTP");
  } catch(e) {
    try {
      xhr = new ActiveXObject("Microsoft.XMLHTTP");
    } catch(e) {
      xhr = false;
    }
  }
}
```

The finished function look like this:

```javascript
function getHTTPObject() {
  var xhr = false;
  if (window.XMLHttpRequest) {
    xhr = new XMLHttpRequest();
  } else if (window.ActiveXObject) {
    try {
      xhr = new ActiveXObject("Msxml2.XMLHTTP");
```

```
  } catch(e) {
    try {
      xhr = new ActiveXObject("Microsoft.XMLHTTP");
    } catch(e) {
      xhr = false;
    }
  }
}
return xhr;
}
```

After all that code forking, you now have a bulletproof way of instantiating an instance of XMLHttpRequest. Don't worry: most of the cross-browser differences end here. Once you've created an object with getHTTPObject, its methods and properties will be the same regardless of whether it's native or an ActiveX object.

Send a Request

Once you have created an instance of XMLHttpRequest, it needs to be prepped for communication with the server. There are three critical components for doing this:

1. The onreadystatechange event handler.

2. The open method.

3. The send method.

ONREADYSTATECHANGE

Event handlers let you specify what behavior should occur when an event is triggered. Most events are triggered by the user. When a user places her cursor over an element in a Web page, the mouseover event for that element is triggered. The corresponding event handler is onmouseover. When a user submits a form, its submit event is fired. The event handler for this is onsubmit.

Event handlers have been crucial to the success of JavaScript on the Web. For years, the most common uses of JavaScript were image rollovers and form validation. Those tasks rely on event handlers such as onmouseover, onmouseout, onblur, onsubmit, and so on.

Not all events are triggered by the user. The load event is fired when a document in the browser window has finished loading. The event handler is window.onload.

The onreadystatechange event handler is rather unusual, and not just because of its ludicrously long name. It is the handler for an event that is triggered not by the user, but by the server.

During an Ajax operation, the server sends updates to the client about the current status of the communication. This is done by updating a property of the XMLHttpRequest object. The property is called readyState, which we'll study in more detail later in this chapter. What interests us now is the fact that every time the readyState property is changed, the readystatechange event is triggered.

Whenever the onreadystatechange event handler captures this event, it means something is happening on the server. Changing the readyState property is the server's way of pinging the client.

If you attach a function to the onreadystatechange event handler, that function will be executed every time the server pings the client with an update. Here's an example:

```
var request = getHTTPObject();
if (request) {
   request.onreadystatechange = doSomething;
}
```

I'm assigning a reference to a function called doSomething to the onreadystatechange event handler. The doSomething function will be executed every time the readystatechange event is triggered.

I've specified what I want to happen when the server sends an update to the client. I still need to specify exactly what I want from the server.

OPEN

When a Web browser asks for a page from a Web server, it issues a request. First and foremost, this request specifies the location of the file on the server that the browser wants to receive. The request might also include more information, such as data inputted through a form. The browser also specifies how the request is sent to the server. This is usually a GET request, unless a lot of data is being sent, in which case the browser uses a POST request.

The open method of the XMLHttpRequest object lets you replicate this kind of transaction in an Ajax call.

This method takes two required arguments:

1. The type of request.

2. The location of the file on the server.

Method

The first argument of the open method is a string such as "GET" or "POST". If you just want to retrieve a file from the server, but you don't need to send any data, use a GET request. If you want to send data to the server, use POST.

GET and POST are examples of request methods, not to be confused with methods of an object. In this sense, *method* simply means the type of request. Other methods include PUT, DELETE, and HEAD.

You can send some data in a GET request by appending a query string to the URL you are requesting. There is a limit on how much data can be sent to the server this way. Also, GET should never be used to send requests that will update something on the server, such as editing or deleting a record in a database.

URL

The second argument of the open method is a string that contains the path to the file on the server that you want to request. This string can be a relative path such as ".../myfile.html" or an absolute path such as "/files/myfile.html".

You could also write out the full path to the file you are requesting:

```
http://www.example.com/files/myfile.html
```

The file you are requesting must reside in the same domain as the JavaScript file that is making the request. If the JavaScript file is being executed from foo.com, it cannot request a file from bar.com. Later on, I will show you some ways of getting around this security restriction, but for now, it's best to think of XMLHttpRequest as being domain-specific.

Asynchronous

As well as the two required parameters, request method and URL, the open method also accepts some optional arguments.

You can specify a Boolean value as the third argument for the open method. This indicates whether the request should occur asynchronously or not.

If you specify a value of `true`, then the script will make an asynchronous request. This means it won't wait for a response from the server before moving on to the rest of the script.

If you specify a value of `false`, then the processing of the script will stop at that point. The script won't resume until the Ajax request is completed.

Halting the execution of a script is rarely a good idea. If the server takes a long time to respond, the browser will effectively stop. One of the great advantages of Ajax is its ability to process requests in the background while the user carries on interacting with the browser. To make use of this, always pass a value of `true` as the third argument in the open method.

Here's a statement that describes an asynchronous GET request to a file in the same directory as the script:

```
request.open("GET", "file.ext", true);
```

User name and password

There are two other optional arguments that you can include in the open method. You can specify a user name and a password to be sent to the server.

Never write sensitive information straight into a JavaScript file. It would be a really bad idea to use the open method like this:

```
request.open("GET", "file.ext", true, "jeremy", "pa55w0rd");
```

Anybody can view the source of a JavaScript file, just as anybody can view the source of a Web page or a CSS file. JavaScript, HTML, and CSS can be obfuscated, but they can never be hidden completely.

You could use the user name and password arguments of the open method to accept values that have been inputted through a form. At least that way, the values aren't hard-coded into a file that's viewable in the browser.

In practice, it is unlikely that you will ever need to make use of these arguments.

SEND

The open method specifies the details of an Ajax request, but it doesn't initiate the request. Use the send method to fire off a request that you have prepared using the open method.

The send method takes a single argument. You can pass it a string of data that will then be sent to the server.

If you are using the GET request method, don't send any data. Instead, pass a value of null to the send method:

```
request.send(null);
```

A complete Ajax GET request looks like this:

```
var request = getHTTPObject();
if (request) {
  request.onreadystatechange = doSomething;
  request.open("GET", "file.ext", true);
  request.send(null);
}
```

If you need to send data to the server, use the POST request method. Send the data as a query string like this:

```
name=Jeremy+Keith&message=Hello+world
```

A query string is made up of name-value pairs joined by ampersands. Each name and value should be URL-encoded. That means spaces become plus signs and non-alphanumeric characters need to be encoded as hex values. The @ symbol becomes %40, for example.

To send data, you need to use one more method of the XMLHttpRequest object.

setRequestHeader

When a Web browser requests a page from a Web server, it sends a series of headers along with the request. These headers are bits of metadata that describe the request. A header is used to declare whether a request is GET or POST.

This ability to send headers can be reproduced in an Ajax request using a method called setRequestHeader. This method accepts two arguments, both of which are strings. The first string specifies the name of the header, and the second string is the value of that header.

If you are sending data to the server with a POST request, you need to set the value of the "Content-type" header to "application/x-www-form-urlencoded":

```
request.setRequestHeader("Content-type", "application/
x-www-form-urlencoded");
```

This lets the server know that data is being sent, and that the data has been URL-encoded.

A complete Ajax POST request looks like this:

```
var request = getHTTPObject();
if (request) {
  request.onreadystatechange = doSomething;
  request.open("POST", "file.ext", true);
  request.setRequestHeader("Content-Type", "application/
x-www-form-urlencoded");
  request.send("name=Jeremy+Keith&message=Hello+world");
}
```

Now you know how to send requests to the server using XMLHttpRequest. Next you'll need to deal with the response from the server.

Receive a Response

Requests are sent to the server using methods of XMLHttpRequest. The object also has a number of properties. Over the course of an Ajax transaction, these properties are updated by the server.

READYSTATE

The readyState property indicates the current state of an Ajax request. Its value is numerical:

- 0 Uninitialized. The open method hasn't been called yet.

- 1 Loading. The open method has been called, but the send method hasn't.

- 2 Loaded. The send method has been called. The request has begun.

- 3 Interactive. The server is in the process of sending a response.

- 4 Complete. The server has finished sending a response.

Every time the value of `readyState` changes, the `readystatechange` event is triggered. If a function has been assigned to the `onreadystatechange` event handler, it will be executed every time `readyState` changes value.

In theory, the value of the `readyState` property will change in numerical order from 0 to 4. In practice, the order in which `readyState` changes varies from browser to browser. Still, every browser finishes with a `readyState` value of 4 when the request is completed.

Rather than trying to do anything clever with the changing `readyState` property, it's best just to wait until its value has reached 4. Then you know the server has finished sending a response.

You can compare the value of the `readyState` property to the number four using a simple `if` statement:

```
function doSomething() {
  if (request.readyState == 4) {
// do something with the response
  }
}
```

The `doSomething` function will be executed more than once because it has been assigned to the `onreadystatechange` event handler:

```
request.onreadystatechange = doSomething;
```

Every time the `readyState` property changes, `doSomething` is executed, but the `if` statement in the function ensures that nothing will happen until `readyState` has a value of 4.

STATUS

In the same way that a Web browser sends headers with each request it makes, a Web server sends headers with each response it sends. These headers contain information about the server, as well as information about the document being served. This information includes the document's content type (HTML, XML, and so on) and character encoding (utf-8, iso-8859-1, and so on).

The most important header sent with any response from a Web server is the status code. This three-digit numerical value, which the server sends with every response to a request, is part of the HyperText Transfer Protocol (HTTP) that drives all communication on the Web. I'm sure you're familiar with the 404 status code, which translates to "Not Found." Some other codes are 403 for "Forbidden," and 500 for "Internal Server Error."

The most common status code is 200, which means "OK." This code indicates that the server successfully sent the requested resource.

In the `XMLHttpRequest` object, the status code sent by the server is available as a property called `status`. By comparing this property to a value of 200, you can be sure that the server has sent a successful response:

```
function doSomething() {
  if (request.readyState == 4) {
    if (request.status == 200) {
// the response was sent successfully
    }
  }
}
```

The first `if` statement within the `doSomething` function compares the `readyState` property to a value of 4. When that evaluates to `true`, meaning that the response is finished being sent, the second `if` statement is executed. This compares the `status` property to a value of 200. If that evaluates to `true`, everything is fine.

By adding an `else` clause, you can also deal with situations where everything doesn't go according to plan:

```
function doSomething() {
  if (request.readyState == 4) {
    if (request.status == 200) {
// the response was sent successfully
    } else {
// something went wrong!
    }
  }
}
```

200 isn't the only server code that indicates a successful response. A value of 304 translates as "Not Modified." The server sometimes returns this response if a browser performs what's known as a conditional GET request. The Opera browser uses conditional GET requests. In this situation, the server may return a response of 304, indicating that the document hasn't changed since it was last requested, so the browser can safely use a cached version.

To accommodate this behavior, test the `status` property for a value of `304`, as well as `200`:

```
function doSomething() {
  if (request.readyState == 4) {
    if (request.status == 200 || request.status == 304) {
// the response was sent successfully
    } else {
// something went wrong!
    }
  }
}
```

RESPONSETEXT

The `responseText` property of `XMLHttpRequest` contains the data sent from the server. It is a string. Depending on what the server is sending, this might be a string of HTML, a string of XML, or just a string of text.

The complete `responseText` property is available when the `readyState` property reaches four, indicating that the Ajax request is complete:

```
function doSomething() {
  if (request.readyState == 4) {
    if (request.status == 200 || request.status == 304) {
      alert(request.responseText);
    }
  }
}
```

In this example, the contents of the `responseText` property will be displayed in an `alert` message.

RESPONSEXML

If the server is sending back XML, then this data will be available in a property called `responseXML`. The `responseXML` property will be available only if the server sends the data with the correct headers. The MIME type must be text/xml.

In the next chapter, I will show you how to parse XML from the `responseXML` property.

Putting It All Together

I'm going to use Ajax to display the contents of a text file. The text file, called `message.txt`, contains a simple line of text:

```
If you can read this, you have successfully requested a text
file from the server.
```

Now I'm going to write a script that will fetch this file and display its contents in an `alert` message. The JavaScript is written in a file called `ajaxtest.js` which is located in the same directory as `message.txt`.

THE JAVASCRIPT

The script begins with the `getHTTPObject` function:

```javascript
function getHTTPObject() {
  var xhr = false;
  if (window.XMLHttpRequest) {
    xhr = new XMLHttpRequest();
  } else if (window.ActiveXObject) {
    try {
      xhr = new ActiveXObject("Msxml2.XMLHTTP");
    } catch(e) {
      try {
        xhr = new ActiveXObject("Microsoft.XMLHTTP");
      } catch(e) {
        xhr = false;
      }
    }
  }
  return xhr;
}
```

Next, write a function called `grabFile`. This function takes a single argument, which is the location of the file I want to display:

```javascript
function grabFile(file) {
}
```

The *grabFile* function begins by creating a new instance of XMLHttpRequest using the getHTTPObject function. If that is successful, then I will initiate an Ajax request:

```
function grabFile(file) {
  var request = getHTTPObject();
  if (request) {
  }
}
```

I want to attach a function called displayResponse to the onreadystatechange event handler. I also want to pass an argument to the displayResponse function, namely the current instance of XMLHttpRequest. To do this, I need to wrap up the call to displayResponse inside an anonymous function:

```
function grabFile(file) {
  var request = getHTTPObject();
  if (request) {
    request.onreadystatechange = function() {
      displayResponse(request);
    };
  }
}
```

Using the send method, I specify the details of the request. This is a GET request; the location of the file being requested is taken from the function's file argument, and the request will be asynchronous:

```
function grabFile(file) {
  var request = getHTTPObject();
  if (request) {
    request.onreadystatechange = function() {
      displayResponse(request);
    };
    request.open("GET", file, true);
  }
}
```

Finally, I set the request in motion using the send method. Because this is a GET request, no data is being sent:

```
function grabFile(file) {
  var request = getHTTPObject();
  if (request) {
    request.onreadystatechange = function() {
      displayResponse(request);
    };
    request.open("GET", file, true);
    request.send(null);
  }
}
```

To handle the response, I need to write the displayResponse function that's referenced from the onreadystatechange event handler. This function takes a single argument, which is an instance of XMLHttpRequest:

```
function displayResponse(request) {
}
```

In this way, the current XMLHttpRequest object can be passed around from function to function.

I don't want to do anything in the displayResponse function until the readyState property has a value of 4:

```
function displayResponse(request) {
  if (request.readyState == 4) {
  }
}
```

I'm also going to check the status property to make sure that the response was successfully returned from the server:

```
function displayResponse(request) {
  if (request.readyState == 4) {
    if (request.status == 200 || request.status == 304) {
    }
  }
}
```

Once these tests have been passed, the responseText property is displayed in an alert message:

```
function displayResponse(request) {
  if (request.readyState == 4) {
    if (request.status == 200 || request.status == 304) {
      alert(request.responseText);
    }
  }
}
```

The script is complete. I need to attach this script to a Web page in order to use it in a browser.

THE MARKUP

Here is a simple XHTML document. The head of the document includes a script element that points to the ajaxtest.js file. The body of the document contains a link to the grabFile function:

```
<!DOCTYPE html PUBLIC "-//W3C//DTD XHTML 1.0 Strict//EN"
"http://www.w3.org/TR/xhtml1/DTD/xhtml1-strict.dtd">
<html>
  <head>
  <title>Using XMLHttpRequest</title>
  <script type="text/javascript" src="ajaxtext.js"></script>
</head>
<body>
  <p>
    <a href="message.txt" onclick="grabFile(this.href);
return false;">
Click here to see the contents of a text file
    </a>
  </p>
</body>
</html>
```

The href attribute of the link points to the message.txt file. An onclick event handler tells the browser to pass this href value to the grabFile function. The return false statement cancels the default behavior, which would be to follow the link in the browser window.

Please bear in mind that this is just an example for testing purposes. Using inline event handlers like this is a crude way of executing JavaScript functions. Later on, you'll see more elegant, advanced ways of adding behavior. For now, this suffices to illustrate basic Ajax functionality.

Save this document as `index.html` in the same directory as `ajaxtest.js` and `message.txt`. In order for this example to work, you'll need to host this directory on a server. This can be your own machine if you are running a Web server locally, or you can transfer the files to a server on the Internet via FTP.

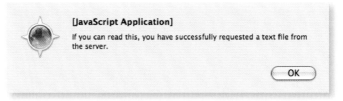

Figure 3.1 A link to a text file.

Navigate to index.html using a Web browser. You will be presented with the link shown in Figure 3.1. Clicking on this link generates the alert dialog shown in Figure 3.2.

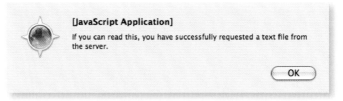

Figure 3.2 The contents of a text file displayed in a dialog.

The content of the alert message comes straight from the message.txt file. On the face of it, this doesn't seem very impressive. There's nothing revolutionary about an alert dialog, but the implications are stunning. It is now possible to take the contents of any file on a server and display its contents in a browser, without refreshing the whole page.

Summary

The XMLHttpRequest object is the heart and soul of Ajax. Its methods and properties drive the asynchronous requests that make Ajax applications feel so responsive.

In this chapter, you've seen how to use the XMLHttpRequest object in three steps:

1. Create an instance of the object that will work across different browser implementations.

2. Prepare a request using the onreadystatechange event handler, the open method, and the send method.

3. Process the response from the server through the properties readyState, status, responseText, and sometimes responseXML.

This basic model will remain unchanged for all the examples throughout this book. The real skill in creating useful Ajax interactivity is deciding where and when to initiate requests and how best to handle the server's response.

In the next chapter, I will look in more detail at the responseText and responseXML properties. These are the carrier mechanisms the server uses to deliver data to the client. That data can be formatted in a number of ways.

Data Formats

4

What's Your Poison?

Ajax is language agnostic, at least on the server. It doesn't matter what server-side language you use for your business logic. However, when you are requesting data from the server, the data that's sent from the server must be formatted in a way that the browser can understand. Your server-side programming language of choice needs to return data in one of three ways: XML, JSON, or HTML. In this chapter, I'm going to examine each data format so that you can make an informed decision as to which one best suits your needs.

XML

Back when the term *AJAX* was an acronym, it stood for Asynchronous JavaScript and XML. *XML* also figures prominently in the name of the `XMLHttpRequest` object. You would be forgiven for thinking that XML is an intrinsic part of Ajax. It isn't. But it can be used as the output format in Ajax responses.

XML stands for eXExtensible Markup Language. It is a general-purpose markup language that can be used to describe just about anything. XML differs from other markup languages like SGML and HTML in that the vocabulary is not prescribed. Instead, the author of an XML document is free to use whatever terms make the most sense to her. It's a kind of metalanguage. The structure of an XML document must follow certain rules, but the vocabulary used within that structure isn't tied to any dictionary of terms.

AN EXAMPLE OF XML

Here is a simple XML document called `jeremy.xml`:

```
<?xml version="1.0" encoding="utf-8"?>
<person>
  <name>Jeremy Keith</name>
  <website>http://adactio.com/</website>
  <email>jeremy@clearleft.com</email>
</person>
```

The first line in the file is an XML declaration. That line states the version of XML being used and the character encoding of the document. Everything after that is contained within tags. Each set of tags denotes an element. The name of an element is contained within the opening and closing tags. The value of an element is also contained between the opening and closing tags.

It's important to note that XML doesn't *do* anything. The language was created as a means of storing data, not manipulating it. In this instance, the XML document is storing contact details for a person. In order to do anything with this data, I'll need to use a programming language. I'm going to use JavaScript to extract the contact information from an XML file and place it into a Web page.

XML IN ACTION

I have a Web page that lists the people in my office. This XHTML document references a JavaScript file called `fetchxml.js` from a `script` element:

```
<!DOCTYPE html PUBLIC "-//W3C//DTD XHTML 1.0 Strict//EN"
"http://www.w3.org/TR/xhtml1/DTD/xhtml1-strict.dtd">
<html xmlns="http://www.w3.org/1999/xhtml" xml:lang="en"
lang="en">  <head>
  <meta http-equiv="content-type" content="text/html;
charset=utf-8" />
  <title>People at Clearleft</title>
  <style type="text/css">
  @import url("clearleft.css");
  </style>
  <script type="text/javascript" src="fetchxml.js"></script>
</head>
<body>
  <h1>People</h1>
  <ul>
    <li>
      <a href="files/andy.xml"
onclick="grabFile(this.href); return false;">Andy</a>
    </li>
    <li>
      <a href="files/richard.xml"
onclick="grabFile(this.href); return false;">Richard</a>
    </li>
    <li>
      <a href="files/jeremy.xml"
onclick="grabFile(this.href); return false;">Jeremy</a>
    </li>
  </ul>
  <div id="details"></div>
</body>
</html>
```

Figure 4.1 shows how this page looks in a browser with some basic styling.

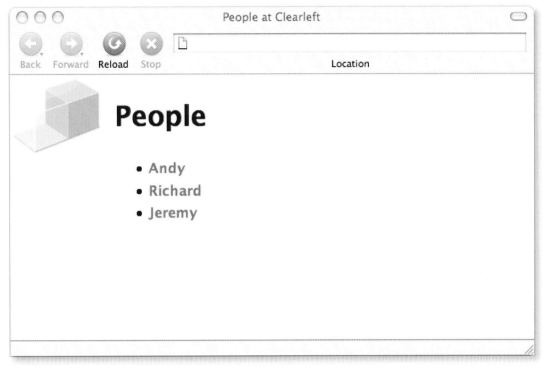

Figure 4.1 A list of people on a Web page.

Each person in the list is linked to the XML file with that person's contact details. I'm using the `onclick` event handler to pass this value to the `grabFile` JavaScript function:

```
<a href="files/jeremy.xml"
onclick="grabFile(this.href); return false;">Jeremy</a>
```

This isn't a very elegant way of capturing events. It's really starting to clutter up the markup. In the next chapter, you'll see a more unobtrusive way of adding JavaScript functionality.

I'm going to write a script that will fetch an XML file, parse its contents, and generate markup to display the contact details in the Web page. These details will go inside the `div` element following the list:

```
<div id="details"></div>
```

Writing the script

The `fetchxml.js` file begins with the `getHTTPObject` function that you saw in the last chapter:

```
function getHTTPObject() {
  var xhr = false;
  if (window.XMLHttpRequest) {
    xhr = new XMLHttpRequest();
  } else if (window.ActiveXObject) {
    try {
      xhr = new ActiveXObject("Msxml2.XMLHTTP");
    } catch(e) {
      try {
        xhr = new ActiveXObject("Microsoft.XMLHTTP");
      } catch(e) {
        xhr = false;
      }
    }
  }
  return xhr;
}
```

That takes care of instantiating a cross-browser `XMLHttpRequest` object.

The next function is `grabFile`. It's almost exactly the same as the `grabFile` function from the last chapter. The only difference is that the `onreadystatechange` event handler now triggers a function called `parseResponse`:

```
function grabFile(file) {
  var request = getHTTPObject();
  if (request) {
    request.onreadystatechange = function() {
      parseResponse(request);
    };
    request.open("GET", file, true);
    request.send(null);
  }
}
```

The `parseResponse` function will take the XML returned from the server and convert it to HTML. But first I need to make sure that the response has been successfully returned from the server:

```
function parseResponse(request) {
  if (request.readyState == 4) {
    if (request.status == 200 || request.status == 304) {
```

The XML is available through the `responseXML` property of the `HTTPRequest` object. I'm going to assign this property to the variable `data`:

```
var data = request.responseXML;
```

The XML can be traversed using the same DOM methods that you would use for traversing an HTML document. As long as you know the structure of the XML being returned from the server, you can get at the information you want using methods like `getElementsByTagName` and properties like `nodeValue`.

Extracting data from XML

I know that there is a `name` element in the XML file. I want to get the text node contained within the `<name>` tags. Using `getElementsByTagName`, I get a collection of all the `name` elements in the XML:
`data.getElementsByTagName("name")`

I know that there is only one `name` element, so I'm only interested in the first occurrence: `data.getElementsByTagName("name")[0]`

This element contains the text node I want. The text node is the first child of the element: `data.getElementsByTagName("name")[0].firstChild`

Now I can get the value of this text node by querying its `nodeValue` property:
`data.getElementsByTagName("name")[0].firstChild.nodeValue`

I'm assigning this value to the variable `name`:

```
var name = data.getElementsByTagName("name")[0].firstChild.
nodeValue;
```

I can use the same DOM methods and properties to retrieve the values in the `website` and `email` elements:

```
var website = data.getElementsByTagName("website")[0].
firstChild.nodeValue;
var email = data.getElementsByTagName("email")[0].
firstChild.nodeValue;
```

The variables name, website, and email contain strings of text retrieved from the corresponding XML elements. Instead of outputting plain text, I want to wrap these values inside HTML elements.

Generating content

Using DOM methods like createElement, createTextNode, and appendChild, I can build up a chunk of HTML to contain the information I have extracted. For instance, I want to output the values of name and email like this:

```
<h2><a href="mailto:jeremy@clearleft.com">Jeremy Keith</a></h2>
```

The h2 and a elements are created with the createElement method:

```
var header = document.createElement("h2");
var mailto = document.createElement("a");
```

I'm using the setAttribute method to give the a element the href value I want:

```
mailto.setAttribute("href","mailto:"+email);
```

Last, I'm using the createTextNode method to create the text to go inside the link:

```
var text = document.createTextNode(name);
```

Now I can use the appendChild method to join these nodes together:

```
mailto.appendChild(text);
header.appendChild(mailto);
```

I also want to output the website value like this:

```
<a href="http://adactio.com/">http://adactio.com/</a>
```

This is accomplished using the same set of DOM methods:

```
var link = document.createElement("a");
link.setAttribute("href",website);
var linktext = document.createTextNode(website);
link.appendChild(linktext);
```

Now I have the HTML I want in the variables header and link. I need to put those elements into the document.

I'm going to insert my newly created markup into the `div` with the ID `details`:

```
var details = document.getElementById("details");
```

First, I'll ensure that this container element is empty:

```
while (details.hasChildNodes()) {
  details.removeChild(details.lastChild);
}
```

The `while` loop will remove the last child until there are no more child nodes left.

Now that the `details` element is empty, I can insert the markup I created:

```
details.appendChild(header);
```

```
details.appendChild(link);
```

That's it. The finished `parseResponse` function looks like this:

```
function parseResponse(request) {
  if (request.readyState == 4) {
    if (request.status == 200 || request.status == 304) {
      var data = request.responseXML;
      var name = data.getElementsByTagName("name")[0].
firstChild.nodeValue;
      var website = data.getElementsByTagName("website")[0].
firstChild.nodeValue;
      var email = data.getElementsByTagName("email")[0].
firstChild.nodeValue;
      var header = document.createElement("h2");
      var mailto = document.createElement("a");
      mailto.setAttribute("href","mailto:"+email);
      var text = document.createTextNode(name);
      mailto.appendChild(text);
      header.appendChild(mailto);
      var link = document.createElement("a");
      link.setAttribute("href",website);
      var linktext = document.createTextNode(website);
      link.appendChild(linktext);
      var details = document.getElementById("details");
      while (details.hasChildNodes()) {
        details.removeChild(details.lastChild);
      }
```

```
        details.appendChild(header);
        details.appendChild(link);
    }
  }
}
```

Save the `fetchxml.js` file and refresh your browser. If you click on one of the links in the document, you will now get the result shown in Figure 4.2.

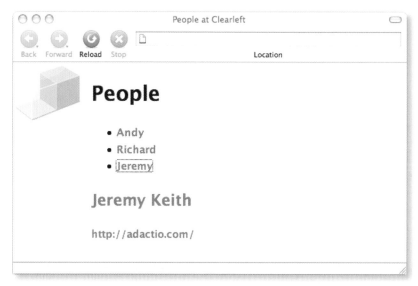

Figure 4.2 Clicking a link displays that person's details.

ADVANTAGES OF XML

XML is a very versatile data format. Instead of forcing your data into predefined fields, you are free to invent a vocabulary to suit your data. This flexibility has helped XML become hugely popular. It is one of the most common means of transferring data within Web applications. That makes it very handy for Ajax applications. If you ask a server-side programmer to return data in XML, your request can be easily met.

The other nice thing about using XML is that you don't need to learn a new language to parse the data. Because the DOM was designed to parse any kind of markup, you can recycle the knowledge that you have already gained from DOM Scripting.

The DOM gives you very fine control over your document. You can extract pieces of data from `responseXML` and then update any part of the current document. In the contact details example, it would be relatively easy to update the `h1` element of the document with the name of the person whose details have been requested:

```
document.getElementsByTagName("h1")[0].firstChild.nodeValue
= name;
```

The precision of the DOM, combined with the popularity of XML, make for a very powerful combination.

DISADVANTAGES OF XML

If you want to send XML from the server, you must ensure that it is sent with the correct headers. If the content type isn't "application/xml," then the `responseXML` property will be empty. If the XML is being generated on the fly by a server-side programming language, it's easy to miss this requirement.

While the DOM is eminently suited to parsing XML once it reaches the browser, it can be a long-winded process. That's evident in the contact details example. It takes quite a few lines of JavaScript just to generate a small chunk of markup. Each node has to be created and appended. For a complex application dealing with longer XML files, the code could quickly get out of hand.

One alternative to using the DOM is XSLT, or eXtensible Stylesheet Language Transformations. This lets you transform XML into HTML by pointing it to a template. Unfortunately, not all browsers support XSLT.

JSON

XML is designed to store data. In order to parse that data, you need some other technology like the DOM or XSLT. Alternatively, you can use a data format that stores data in a way that makes it easier for programming languages to parse.

JSON, which stands for JavaScript Object Notation, is pronounced like the name Jason. Incidentally, in Greek mythology, one of Jason's Argonauts was Telamon, father of Ajax.

JSON is the brainchild of Douglas Crockford, one of the preeminent JavaScript coders in the world today (www.crockford.com).

Crockford proposes JSON as a lightweight alternative to XML. Anything that can be stored in XML can also be stored in JSON. Both are text-based representations of data, but while XML requires opening and closing tags, JSON just uses colons, commas, and curly braces.

JSON isn't a data format that needs to be interpreted by JavaScript: JSON *is* JavaScript.

AN EXAMPLE OF JSON

As you've already seen, there's always more than one way of doing something in JavaScript. Take this function declaration, for example:

```
function person() {
  var name = "Richard Rutter";
  var website = "http://clagnut.com/";
  var email = "richard@clearleft.com";
}
```

This function isn't very useful for achieving a task, but it is a handy way of storing data in a single global variable. It could also be written like this:

```
var person = function() {
  var name = "Richard Rutter";
  var website = "http://clagnut.com/";
  var email = "richard@clearleft.com";
};
```

In order to access all those local variables from outside the function, turn person into an object:

```
var person = function() {
  this.name = "Richard Rutter";
  this.website = "http://clagnut.com/";
  this.email = "richard@clearleft.com";
};
```

Now name, website, and email are available as properties of person: person.name, person.website, and person.email.

That same object can be written like this:

```
{"person":{
  "name":"Richard Rutter",
  "website":"http://clagnut.com/",
  "email":"richard@clearleft.com"
  }
}
```

This is called an object literal. Values are assigned using colons instead of equals signs. Each assignment is separated with a comma. The whole object is encapsulated within curly braces. More sets of curly braces can be used to nest more levels of information.

The values stored in an object literal can be strings, numbers, or Boolean values. Object literals can also store functions, which are methods of the object. But if you write an object literal purely for storing data, then you are writing JSON.

JSON IN ACTION

Returning to the contact details page, I'm going to change the links to point to JSON files:

```
<!DOCTYPE html PUBLIC "-//W3C//DTD XHTML 1.0 Strict//EN"
"http://www.w3.org/TR/xhtml1/DTD/xhtml1-strict.dtd">
<html xmlns="http://www.w3.org/1999/xhtml" xml:lang="en"
lang="en">  <head>
  <meta http-equiv="content-type" content="text/html;
charset=utf-8" />
  <title>People at Clearleft</title>
  <style type="text/css">
  @import url("clearleft.css");
  </style>
  <script type="text/javascript" src="fetchjson.js"></
script>
</head>
<body>
  <h1>People</h1>
  <ul>
    <li>
```

```
      <a href="files/andy.js"
onclick="grabFile(this.href); return false;">Andy</a>
    </li>
    <li>
      <a href="files/richard.js"
onclick="grabFile(this.href); return false;">Richard</a>
    </li>
    <li>
      <a href="files/jeremy.js"
onclick="grabFile(this.href); return false;">Jeremy</a>
    </li>
  </ul>
  <div id="details"></div>
</body>
</html>
```

The script element now points to a file called `fetchjson.js`. This is very similar to the `fetchxml.js` file I've already written. The functions `getHTTPObject` and `grabFile` are exactly the same. All I need to change is the `parseResponse` function.

Extracting data from JSON

When my data was stored in XML, I was parsing the `responseXML` property. JSON is simply a string of text. It is returned in the `responseText` property.

To access JSON data stored in the `responseText` property, I need to use JavaScript's `eval` statement. The `eval` function accepts a string as an argument. This string is then executed as JavaScript code. Because a string of JSON consists of JavaScript code, it can be evaluated.

Here, I'm evaluating the contents of the `responseText` property and assigning the result to the variable `data`:

```
var data = eval('('+request.responseText+')');
```

Now I can access all of the JSON values as properties of `data`:

```
var name = data.person.name;
var email = data.person.email;
var website = data.person.website;
```

This dot syntax is shorter and more readable than the DOM methods I used on the XML files:

```
var name = data.getElementsByTagName("name")[0].firstChild.
nodeValue;
```

Once the data has been extracted, the `parseResponse` function continues exactly as before, generating markup and inserting it into the document:

```
function parseResponse(request) {
  if (request.readyState == 4) {
    if (request.status == 200 || request.status == 304) {
      var data = eval('('+request.responseText+')');
      var name = data.person.name;
      var email = data.person.email;
      var website = data.person.website;
      var header = document.createElement("h2");
      var mailto = document.createElement("a");
      mailto.setAttribute("href","mailto:"+email);
      var text = document.createTextNode(name);
      mailto.appendChild(text);
      header.appendChild(mailto);
      var link = document.createElement("a");
      link.setAttribute("href",website);
      var linktext = document.createTextNode(website);
      link.appendChild(linktext);
      var details = document.getElementById("details");
      while (details.hasChildNodes()) {
        details.removeChild(details.lastChild);
      }
      details.appendChild(header);
      details.appendChild(link);
    }
  }
}
```

The final result is the same, as shown in Figure 4.3.

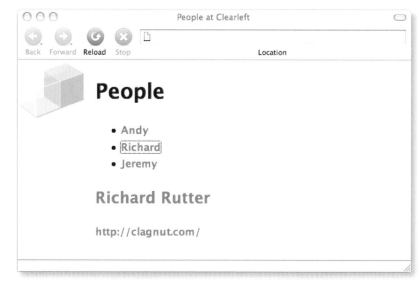

Figure 4.3 JSON is converted into HTML.

As you can see, there isn't much difference between JSON and XML when you're using XMLHttpRequest to send data from your server.

If we take XMLHttpRequest out of the equation, JSON has one huge advantage as a data format: you can request JSON data from a remote server.

THE SCRIPT TAG HACK

Security restrictions prevent us from using XMLHttpRequest to access any domain other than the one serving up the JavaScript file being executed. This means we can't access remote servers like this:

```
request.open("GET", "http://api.search.yahoo.com/", true);
```

We can't use XMLHttpRequest to access the Web APIs offered by so many sites these days. That's a real shame because most APIs return their data in XML, which would then be available in responseXML.

The script element has no such security restrictions. It's possible to access a JavaScript file from another domain in this way:

```
<script type="text/javascript"
src="http://www.google-analytics.com/urchin.js"></script>
```

If you can request a JavaScript file from another domain, then you can also request a JSON file. Remember, JSON is nothing more than JavaScript.

Using some DOM Scripting, you can dynamically generate a `script` element. This function accepts a URL as its argument. It creates a new `script` element with the URL as its `src` attribute, and then adds the element to the `head` of the document:

```
function getScript(url) {
  var scripttag = document.createElement("script");
  scripttag.setAttribute("type","text/javascript");
  scripttag.setAttribute("src",url);
  document.getElementsByTagName("head")[0].
appendChild(scripttag);
}
```

JSON and Web Services

Some APIs now offer JSON as an alternative to XML. All of Yahoo's Web Services can return JSON if it's requested. If you'd like to try using the Yahoo Search API, sign up for an application ID at http://api.search.yahoo.com/webservices/register_application.

My own application ID is adactio. Substitute your own ID in this function:

```
function searchYahoo(query) {
  var url = "http://api.search.yahoo.com/NewsSearchService/
V1/newsSearch?";
  url+= "appid=adactio";
  url+= "&query="+escape(query);
  url+= "&output=json";
  url+= "&callback=parseResponse";
  getScript(url);
}
```

The searchYahoo function puts together a URL with the required parameters for a search. The search term itself is passed as an argument, query. The other required parameter is the application ID, appid.

There are two optional parameters added to the URL. The first, output, is given a value of json, indicating that the results should be returned in JSON rather than XML. The other parameter, callback, indicates that the JSON data should be evaluated and passed to the function parseResponse.

By passing this URL to the `getScript` function, this kind of JSON is retrieved from Yahoo:

```
{"ResultSet":
  {
  "totalResultsAvailable":2,
  "totalResultsReturned":2,
  "firstResultPosition":"1",
  "Result":[
    {
    "Title":"Man Bites Dog",
    "Summary":"Headline writers take the day off.",
    "Url":"http://www.example.com/false.html"
    },
    {
    "Title":"Stop The Press",
    "Summary":"Man injured by spinning newspaper.",
    "Url":"http://www.example.com/fake.html"
    }
  ]}
}
```

That information can then be parsed in the `parseResponse` function:

```
function parseResponse(data) {
  for (var i=0; i<data.ResultSet.Result.length; i++) {
    var title = data.ResultSet.Result[i].Title;
    var summary = data.ResultSet.Result[i].Summary;
    var url = data.ResultSet.Result[i].Url;
  }
}
```

You can trigger the `searchYahoo` function from a Web page like this:

```
<!DOCTYPE html PUBLIC "-//W3C//DTD XHTML 1.0 Strict//EN"
"http://www.w3.org/TR/xhtml1/DTD/xhtml1-strict.dtd">
<html xmlns="http://www.w3.org/1999/xhtml" xml:lang="en"
lang="en">
<head>
  <title>Yahoo! News Search</title>
  <script type="text/javascript" src="jsonsearch.js">
  </script>
```

```
  <style type="text/css">
  @import url("style.css");
  </style>
</head>
<body>
  <h1>Yahoo! News Search</h1>
  <form onsubmit="searchYahoo(this.query.value); return
false">
    <fieldset>
      <label>Search for</label>
      <input type="text" name="query" />
      <input type="submit" value="Search"  />
    </fieldset>
  </form>
  <div id="results"></div>
</body>
</html>
```

Put the getScript and searchYahoo functions in the jsonsearch.js file.
You'll also need to write an expanded version of parseResponse.

This will convert the search results into HTML and place them inside the
element with the ID results:

```
function parseResponse(data) {
// empty the div
  var results = document.getElementById("results");
  while (results.hasChildNodes()) {
    results.removeChild(results.lastChild);
  }
// loop through the search results
  for (var i=0; i<data.ResultSet.Result.length; i++) {
    var title = data.ResultSet.Result[i].Title;
    var summary = data.ResultSet.Result[i].Summary;
    var url = data.ResultSet.Result[i].Url;
// create the headline link
    var header = document.createElement("h2");
    var link = document.createElement("a");
    link.setAttribute("href",url);
    var text = document.createTextNode(title);
    link.appendChild(text);
    header.appendChild(link);
```

```
// create the summary paragraph
    var para = document.createElement("p");
    var paratext = document.createTextNode(summary);
    para.appendChild(paratext);
// insert the markup
    results.appendChild(header);
    results.appendChild(para);
  }
}
```

Try typing in a search to see the results, as shown in Figure 4.4.

Figure 4.4 Search results for *Google* from Yahoo News.

ADVANTAGES OF JSON

As a format for transmitting data, JSON is quite similar to XML, but it is a bit more lightweight. Whereas every value in XML requires an opening and a closing tag, JSON only requires a name to be written once.

Unlike XML, JSON doesn't need to be sent from the server with a specific content-type header. It can be sent as plain text.

JSON's greatest asset is its ability to travel across domains. This means abandoning the `XMLHttpRequest` object in favor of the script tag hack, but right now, that's the only way of directly retrieving data from another server.

DISADVANTAGES OF JSON

JSON's syntax is very precise. One misplaced comma or missing curly brace will put paid to an entire JSON object. You must also remember to escape special characters such as quotation marks.

Unlike Douglas Crockford, I don't find JSON to be very readable. Perhaps it's because I'm used to angle brackets in HTML, but XML's tag-based syntax looks cleaner to me.

In order to extract the contents of a JSON object, it must be evaluated. The `eval` function is powerful, and potentially dangerous. If you're retrieving JSON data from a third party that isn't entirely trustworthy, it could contain some malicious JavaScript code that will be executed with `eval`. For this reason, Douglas Crockford has written a JSON parser that will parse only properties, ignoring any methods (www.json.org/js.html).

HTML

If you are sending data as XML or JSON, you need to convert it into HTML before displaying it in a Web browser. This extra step can be avoided if data is sent as HTML to begin with.

AN EXAMPLE OF HTML

For the contact details page, data can be sent back like this:

```
<h2><a href="mailto:andy@clearleft.com">Andy Budd</a></h2>
<a href="http://andybudd.com/">http://andybudd.com/</a>
```

Technically, this isn't an HTML file. There is no doctype declaration. There is no `body` element, no `head` element, or even an `html` element. It would be more accurate to call this a fragment or a snippet of HTML.

This fragment is ready to be inserted into the current document as it is.

HTML IN ACTION

I have updated the contact details page to point to a JavaScript file called `fetchhtml.js`:

```
<script type="text/javascript" src="fetchhtml.js"></script>
```

I'm also changing the markup so that the links now point to the snippets of HTML with each person's contact details:

```
<ul>
  <li>
    <a href="files/andy.html"
onclick="grabFile(this.href); return false;">Andy</a>
  </li>
  <li>
    <a href="files/richard.html"
onclick="grabFile(this.href); return false;">Richard</a>
  </li>
  <li>
    <a href="files/jeremy.html"
onclick="grabFile(this.href); return false;">Jeremy</a>
  </li>
</ul>
<div id="details"></div>
```

In the `fetchhtml.js` file, the `getHTTPObject` stays the same. So does the `grabFile` function. All I need to update is the `parseResponse` function.

Extracting Data from HTML

HTML consists of plain text. If the server sends HTML via `XMLHttpRequest`, it will be available in the `responseText` property.

I don't need to extract any data from `responseText`. It's already preformatted just the way I want it. All I need to do is dump it into the part of the page that I want to update.

In this case, I want to update the `div` with the ID `details`:

```
var details = document.getElementById("details");
```

The simplest way of inserting a fragment of HTML is to update this element's `innerHTML` property.

innerHTML

The `innerHTML` property is not part of the DOM. It isn't part of any standard. It is a proprietary addition created by Microsoft.

Normally, I wouldn't recommend using anything proprietary in your JavaScript code (although the `XMLHttpRequest` object itself is a proprietary addition). However, the `innerHTML` property is exceptionally well supported, considering that it is nonstandard. It is, in effect, a de facto standard: it is supported in all the major browsers. The reason why `innerHTML` has been so widely adopted, without any endorsement from the W3C, is that it is very useful in certain situations.

DOM methods allow you to manipulate a document very precisely. You can create elements, attributes, and text, one node at a time. That is very powerful, but it is also quite time-consuming.

The `innerHTML` property uses brute force. If you read the `innerHTML` property of an element, you will receive a string of HTML. This is a read/write property, meaning that you can also assign a string of HTML to go inside an element:

```
element.innerHTML = "<p>Here's a string of markup.</p>";
```

Any HTML that was previously inside the element will be obliterated and replaced with the contents of the string.

If you use DOM methods like `createElement`, `createTextNode`, and `appendChild`, you cannot create badly formed markup. If you assign a badly formed string of HTML to an element's `innerHTML` property, you will mess up your document's DOM tree:

```
element.innerHTML = "<p>This is <em>badly formed</p></em>";
```

When it's used carelessly, `innerHTML` can be very dangerous. But it can be a real time-saver. Not only does assigning an `innerHTML` value take less time than creating and appending nodes one by one, it's also a much faster way of updating a document. This difference in speed varies from browser to browser, but it becomes noticeable when you're dealing with very large chunks of markup.

I'm going to update the `parseResponse` function to change the `innerHTML` property of the `details` element:

```
function parseResponse(request) {
  if (request.readyState == 4) {
    if (request.status == 200 || request.status == 304) {
      var details = document.getElementById("details");
      details.innerHTML = request.responseText;
    }
  }
}
```

That's it. With one statement I can update the document with the markup returned from the server.

Click on any of the links on the contact details page to get the desired result, as shown in Figure 4.5.

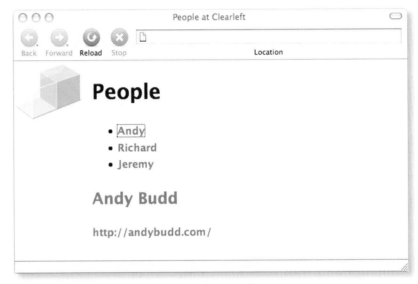

Figure 4.5 Updating a document with HTML fragments.

ADVANTAGES OF HTML

Sending HTML fragments from the server can save a lot of time in the browser. You don't need to write lines and lines of JavaScript to parse the response and convert it into HTML. The data is already formatted in HTML and only needs to be inserted into the document. This can be accomplished in a single line using `innerHTML`. That can result in a significant saving in your script's file size.

As a data format, HTML fragments are certainly as readable as XML or JSON—perhaps more so, given the ubiquity of HTML on the Web and its familiarity to developers.

Using HTML fragments together with the `innerHTML` property is a fast and efficient combination.

DISADVANTAGES OF HTML

Sending an HTML fragment in an Ajax response works well if you want to update one part of a document. It doesn't work so well if you want to update multiple parts of the same document. In such cases, it's better to use a data format like XML or JSON, which can be parsed very precisely.

Perhaps the biggest problem with using HTML fragments is the reliance on `innerHTML`. As a dyed-in-the-wool standardista, I'm not entirely comfortable with using a nonstandard property.

Technically, the `innerHTML` property should work only in HTML documents, not in XHTML documents. If you are going to be pedantic, you should be serving up XHTML pages with a content-type header of `application/xhtml+xml`. But if you do that, you can't use `innerHTML` in older versions of Firefox. In practice, most people serve up XHTML as HTML because Internet Explorer can't handle the correct content-type header.

Summary

In this chapter, you've seen three ways of formatting information returned from the server in an Ajax response. Each format has its strengths and weaknesses.

- XML is a popular format that can be parsed using the DOM.

- JSON can be used to retrieve data from a remote server, if you use the script tag hack.

- HTML fragments can be dumped straight into a page using `innerHTML`.

In my experience, using HTML fragments is often the quickest and easiest way of updating part of a page without refreshing the whole page. Most of the examples I'll be showing you from now on will use this solution.

All of the examples I've shown you so far have worked fine, but they aren't very elegant. I've been embedding event handlers in my markup to trigger JavaScript functions. If JavaScript is switched off, there is no fallback functionality. That's not very bulletproof.

In the next chapter, I'm going to show you how this can be fixed. We will examine the concepts of progressive enhancement and unobtrusive JavaScript, and see how those ideas can be applied to Ajax.

5

Hijax

The Secret of Your Success

JavaScript is a great programming language, but it isn't ubiquitous. Although all modern browsers support JavaScript, older browsers don't. Even when JavaScript is supported, users can always choose to disable it. They might do this to comply with a workplace policy, or simply to avoid the annoyance of pop-up windows.

If JavaScript is not available, then neither is Ajax. This is the Achilles' heel of many Ajax applications. Without JavaScript, the application ceases to work.

To offset this weakness, some applications offer a separate non-Ajax version. Creating a simpler version inevitably takes a lot of time and effort. This solution is similar to providing a text-only version of a Web site to meet accessibility requirements. This "separate but equal" approach leads to the fragmentation of features and the ghettoization of users.

Ideally, a Web site should be able to adapt to the needs and capabilities of a browser or user without splitting into separate, difficult-to-maintain versions.

Progressive Enhancement

Progressive enhancement is a Web-design strategy in which features are prioritized in order of importance. For instance, the content of a Web document is its most important component. Therefore, the content should be available to the widest number of devices possible. The visual design of a Web page is important, but not as critical as the content, since it is layered on top of the content. Some browsers will not receive the page with the desired visual design, but all browsers will receive the content.

By layering on enhancements like this, you can create a single Web site that uses as many features as the browser permits. The crucial point is that you add each layer of enhancement separately, so that the layers are not dependent on each other.

LEARNING FROM CSS

Cascading Style Sheets (CSS) are well suited to the principle of progressive enhancement. Style declarations can be layered on top of existing markup. CSS-capable browsers display the content with the declarations applied. If CSS is not supported, the content is still available.

Figure 5.1 illustrates how my Web site looks in a CSS-capable browser.

Figure 5.2 shows the same site with styles disabled.

The only requirement for viewing the content is that the browser understands HTML or XHTML. Because the CSS is layered on top of the markup, I don't have to create a separate, simpler version for older browsers. One size fits all.

Another great advantage of CSS is that style declarations can be stored in external files. Instead of setting style declarations inside HTML tags, it makes more sense to keep all your style information in a centralized place. This keeps your markup nice and clean, making it easier to update the content. It's also easier to update an external style sheet than to wade through a mishmash of markup and CSS in search of one elusive declaration.

Figure 5.1 My site, adactio.com, is enhanced with CSS.

Figure 5.2 Here is adactio.com laid bare.

Unobtrusive JavaScript

As with CSS, it really pays to keep your JavaScript in external files rather than in your markup. Most scripts are written and stored in external .js files that are referenced from Web pages using `<script>` tags. Still, some JavaScript remains mingled with the markup.

JavaScript functions are sometimes triggered from a link using the `javascript:` pseudo-protocol, like this:

```
<a href="javascript:doSomething();">Click me!</a>
```

This is not a real Internet protocol like `http://` or `ftp://`. It presupposes support for JavaScript. If JavaScript isn't enabled, at best nothing happens. At worst, the browser throws an error.

More commonly, JavaScript calls are placed in event-handling attributes like `onclick`. All too often, these event handlers are associated with a pointless internal link:

```
<a href="#" onclick="doSomething(); return false;">Click
me!</a>
```

This is slightly better than using the `javascript:` pseudo-protocol, but it's still an abuse of the `href` attribute. If JavaScript is disabled, the user is sent to the top of the current document.

The `href` attribute should contain a reference to a real resource. This can act as a fallback if JavaScript is not available:

```
<a href="page.html" onclick="doSomething(); return
false;">Click me!</a>
```

This technique doesn't assume that JavaScript will always be available. That's a key difference compared with the `javascript:` pseudo-protocol. But it still places calls to JavaScript functions inside inline event handlers. That's the scripting equivalent to using inline styles for CSS. Ideally, markup and JavaScript should be kept separate. That goal can be achieved through the practice of *unobtrusive JavaScript*.

EVENT HANDLING

You don't need to use inline event handlers to trigger JavaScript functions. You can attach functions to events using some DOM Scripting.

An event is always attached to an element. Using DOM methods like getElementById and getElementsByTagName, it is relatively easy to find a specific element or elements. Every element comes with a range of event-handling properties: onclick, onmouseover, onmouseout, and so on. If you assign a function to one of these events, the function will be executed when the event is triggered.

The following assigns the doSomething function to the click event of every link in the document:

```
var links = document.getElementsByTagName("a");
for (var i=0; i<links.length; i++) {
  links[i].onclick = function() {
    doSomething();
    return false;
  };
}
```

I'm using an anonymous function to store the actions that should be triggered by the click event. I could have passed a reference to a function instead:

```
links[i].onclick = doSomething;
```

In that case, I would need to make sure that the doSomething function returned a value of false to prevent the browser from actually following the link.

This won't work:

```
links[i].onclick = doSomething();
```

Instead of assigning the doSomething function to the onclick event handler, the function will be executed immediately. When you assign functions to an event handler, you need to either pass a function reference (without parentheses) or assign an anonymous function.

We want to get loaded

There's one problem with using external rather than inline event handlers. Whenever you use DOM methods, there must be a complete Document Object Model. If the document hasn't completely loaded, the DOM is incomplete.

When a browser fetches a Web page from a server, it parses the page from top to bottom, building a node tree as it goes. As it works its way through the head element, it may come across a <script> tag that points to an external JavaScript file. The browser now fetches this JavaScript file and begins executing it, top to bottom. If a JavaScript statement makes use of getElementsByTagName or getElementById, the browser can't find the elements being sought. It hasn't finished loading the document.

This brings back no results:

```
var links = document.getElementsByTagName("a");
```

The browser has yet to encounter a single a element.

If you want to use DOM methods, you must wait until the document has finished loading. Fortunately, this is easily accomplished by assigning functions to the load event of the window object:

```
window.onload = prepareLinks;
function prepareLinks() {
  var links = document.getElementsByTagName("a");
  for (var i=0; i<links.length; i++) {
    links[i].onclick = function() {
      doSomething();
      return false;
    };
  }
}
```

This assigns the prepareLinks function to the window.onload event handler.

One problem with using window.onload is that you can assign only one value to it. It is likely that you will want to queue up quite a few functions to be executed when the document loads. To help you do that, you can use the addLoadEvent function:

```
function addLoadEvent(func) {
  var oldonload = window.onload;
  if (typeof window.onload != 'function') {
    window.onload = func;
  } else {
    window.onload = function() {
      if (oldonload) {
        oldonload();
      }
      func();
```

```
      }
    }
}
```

This handy little function was written by Simon Willison (http://simon willison.net/). It takes a single argument, which is a reference to a function you would like to execute once the document has finished loading:

`addLoadEvent(prepareLinks);`

The `prepareLinks` function is added to the list of functions that will be executed when the document has loaded.

An alternative to triggering functions with the `window.onload` event handler is to place your `<script>` tags right before the closing `</body>` tag. You can then execute your functions immediately because the DOM will be (mostly) complete.

Progressive Enhancement and Ajax

When the principle of progressive enhancement is applied to DOM Scripting, the result is unobtrusive JavaScript. Scripting enhancements, contained in external JavaScript files, are applied to a document without ever assuming that JavaScript will be present. If JavaScript is unavailable, the content of the document is still available and all its links and forms still work. If JavaScript is available, extra functionality is added with DOM Scripting. Most importantly, none of this added functionality is mission critical.

After many years of irresponsible scripting, this approach to JavaScript is gaining some ground, particularly among standards-savvy front-end developers who have experienced the benefits of progressive enhancement with CSS.

Alas, the advent of Ajax may have turned back the clock.

Far too many Ajax applications are built on the assumption that JavaScript will be available. Instead of treating the language as a tool for enhancing functionality, these applications make JavaScript a requirement. Core functionality is carried out with JavaScript, resulting in an all-or-nothing situation for the user. The only option is to waste time and energy building a separate, plain vanilla version without JavaScript.

This problem can be avoided by applying the principle of progressive enhancement to Ajax.

THE HIJAX APPROACH

I'd like to introduce you to a methodology I call Hijax. It's a two-step plan for building Ajax applications that degrade gracefully:

1. Begin by building a regular Web page. The user can request information from and send information to the server using links and forms. The server returns an updated version of the same page. Every time the user clicks on a link or submits a form, the entire page is refreshed.

2. Use DOM Scripting to intercept (or hijack) the links and forms that are requesting information from and sending information to the server. Reroute these requests through the `XMLHttpRequest` object. Instead of returning the entire page, the server just needs to send back the part of the page that changes.

Step 1 doesn't require JavaScript, CSS, or any other client-side technology. All the processing takes place on the server.

In Step 2, JavaScript is used to enhance the user experience. Instead of refreshing the whole page, only part of the page is updated. It's important to note that all of the processing still takes place on the server.

The `XMLHttpRequest` object acts like a dumbwaiter. It shuttles data to and from the browser, but the business logic remains firmly on the server.

It is not a good idea to entrust core functionality to a client-side scripting language. The browser is an unpredictable environment. You can't be certain what kind of browsers your visitors will be using, or whether JavaScript will be turned on in those browsers. Your server environment is much more predictable. You know its capabilities. You know what languages it can execute. Wherever possible, get the server, not the browser, to do the important work.

ARCHITECTURE

In order for the Hijax technique to work well, pages should be constructed on the server in a modular fashion. This is how most Web pages are put together nowadays.

A typical Web page is made up of a collection of components. Some of these components, like the branding, the navigation, and the fine print at the bottom of the page, are constant from page to page. Other components, like the body copy, are page specific.

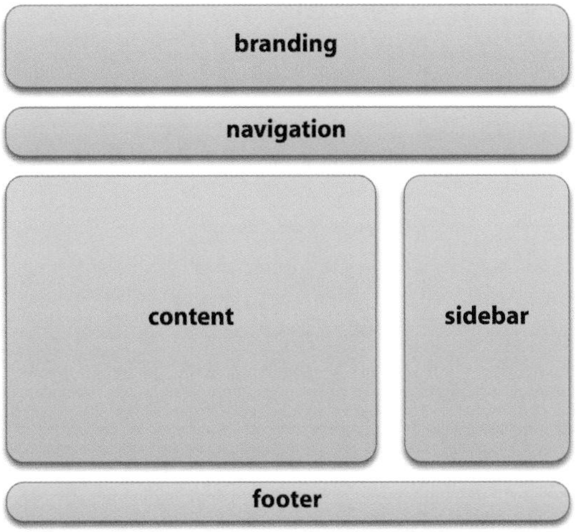

Figure 5.3 Here's the architecture of a typical Web page.

The components that are reused from page to page are usually kept in separate files. There's one file for displaying the navigation and another for displaying the footer. When a page is requested, the server pulls in these reusable files and integrates them with the page-specific content. Quite often, this content is extracted from a database.

Here is the skeletal markup of a typical page:

```
<!-- doctype -->
<html>
<head>
  <title><!-- page title --></title>
  <!-- fetch stylesheets and scripts -->
</head>
<body>
  <div id="branding"><!-- display branding --></div>
  <div id="navigation"><!-- display navigation --></div>
  <div id="content">
  <!-- display content from a database -->
  </div>
  <div id="sidebar"><!-- display sidebar --></div>
  <div id="footer"><!-- display footer --></div>
</body>
</html>
```

Figure 5.4 Here are subcomponents you might find in a sidebar.

Notice that the separate components are often contained within <div> tags. The div element has something of a bad reputation because it is often over-used. But it does have some semantic meaning: it defines a self-contained section, or division, of a Web page. These divisions can continue down to a finer level. A sidebar, for example, might contain subcomponents like a log-in form or a shopping cart.

These subcomponents are generated on the server, based on the user's actions. They are ideal candidates for Hijax. They would probably be contained in their own div elements:

```
<div id="sidebar">
  <div id="login"><!-- display login form --></div>
  <div id="cart"><!-- display shopping cart --></div>
</div>
```

The planning paradox

There seems to be a contradiction in what I'm suggesting. On the one hand, I'm advocating building an old-fashioned Web site to begin with, instead of starting with the assumption that Ajax will drive the interaction. On the other hand, it's clear that if you want to use Ajax effectively, the back-end architecture of your Web site needs to be very modular. That's something that needs to be planned from the start.

This paradox can be resolved by following these two guidelines:

1. Plan for Ajax from the start.

2. Implement Ajax at the end.

Thinking about Ajax interactivity at the beginning of a project encourages you to view your pages as a collection of modules, some of which could benefit from Ajax. But instead of diving right in with Ajax when it comes time to build these pages, it pays to start by using regular page-based interaction. If you do that, then you know your site will be backward-compatible. You won't have to build a separate non-Ajax version; it will already exist. All you have to do is apply Ajax functionality using the principle of progressive enhancement.

PATTERN RECOGNITION

Think about situations that fulfill these criteria:

1. The server sends a Web page to a browser.

2. The user can fill in a form or click on a link with a query string.

3. The server sends the same page back to the browser. Part of the page has been changed based on the user's request.

Using Hijax, you can change Step 3. Instead of requesting the entire page, use Ajax to request only the updated component.

Hijax in Action

I'm going to revisit the contact details page from Chapter 4. I need to start over. First of all, I'm going to build this page so that it works without JavaScript.

The links now pass a parameter called person in a query string to the same page:

```
<ul>
  <li>
    <a href="?person=andy">Andy</a>
  </li>
  <li>
    <a href="?person=richard">Richard</a>
  </li>
  <li>
    <a href="?person=jeremy">Jeremy</a>
  </li>
</ul>
```

I'm changing this page from a static HTML file into a dynamic PHP file. You can use any server-side programming language to handle the parameter being passed. I'm using PHP because that's what I'm comfortable with.

Inside the "details" div, I'm including a PHP file called people.php:

```
<div id="details">
<?php include "people.php"; ?>
</div>
```

This file contains a simple bit of PHP. It checks to see if the parameter `person` has been sent in the query string. If it has, the appropriate markup is displayed:

```php
<?php
if (isset($_GET["person"])) {
  switch ($_GET["person"]) {
    case "andy":
      include "files/andy.html";
    break;
    case "richard":
      include "files/richard.html";
    break;
    case "jeremy":
      include "files/jeremy.html";
    break;
  }
}
?>
```

This is a small, self-contained script. In a real-world situation, it would probably be more complex. Scripts like this might extract contact details from a database or by parsing an XML file. The end result is the same. The file displays some HTML with a person's contact details.

The markup that gets displayed looks like this:

```html
<h2><a href="mailto:jeremy@clearleft.com">Jeremy Keith</a>
</h2>
<a href="http://adactio.com/">http://adactio.com/</a>
```

Clicking on any name in the list refreshes the page and displays the contact details for that person. Everything works fine without JavaScript.

Next, I'm going to layer some Ajax on top of the existing functionality. When a person's name is clicked, I want to display his details without refreshing the whole page. To do that, I need to intercept the default browser behavior and replace it with the behavior I want.

CAPTURING LINK DATA

First I need to hijack the links in the list of people's names. This is easy to do with the DOM if the list has a unique ID. I'm giving the list an ID of people. Here's the basic page structure:

```
<h1>People</h1>
<ul id="people">
...
</ul>
<div id="details">
...
</div>
```

Now I have easy access to all the links in the list, using a combination of getElementById and getElementsByTagName.

In an external JavaScript file called ajax.js, I have a function called prepareLinks:

```
function prepareLinks() {
```

First, I'm going to use object detection to make sure that the browser understands the DOM methods I'm going to employ:

```
if (!document.getElementById || !document.
getElementsByTagName) {
   return;
}
```

To be on the safe side, I'm going to make sure that the "people" list exists before I attempt to do anything with it:

```
if (!document.getElementById("people")) {
   return;
}
```

I begin by getting all the links in the "people" list:

```
var list = document.getElementById("people");
var links = list.getElementsByTagName("a");
```

I'm looping through each of these links and attaching an anonymous function to its onclick event handler:

```
for (var i=0; i<links.length; i++) {
  links[i].onclick = function() {
```

When the link is clicked, I want to extract the query string from its `href` attribute. I can do this using JavaScript's `split` function, which splits a string into an array. I'm going to split the `href` attribute on the question mark character. The first member in the resulting array will be everything before the question mark. This has an index of zero. The second member, which has an index of one, contains everything after the question mark:

```
var query = this.getAttribute("href").split("?")[1];
```

Now I can construct the URL that I want for my Ajax request. I'm requesting the file `people.php`, followed by a question mark, followed by the query string I've just extracted:

```
var url = "people.php?"+query;
```

This is the value I'm going to pass to the `grabFile` function that we wrote in Chapter 4:

```
grabFile(url);
```

I'm going to change the `grabFile` function slightly. It will return a value of `true` if the browser is Ajax capable, and `false` otherwise. To stop the page from refreshing, I'm going use this returned value. If `grabFile` returns a value of `true`, then I will cancel the default browser behavior for the `click` event like this:

```
return !grabFile(url);
```

This statement returns the opposite of whatever `grabFile` returns. If `grabFile` returns true, this returns false, thereby canceling the default browser behavior. But if `grabFile` returns false, this statement returns true and the browser will follow the link.

The finished function looks like this:

```
function prepareLinks() {
  if (!document.getElementById || !document.
getElementsByTagName) {
    return;
  }
  if (!document.getElementById("people")) {
    return;
  }
  var list = document.getElementById("people");
  var links = list.getElementsByTagName("a");
```

```
  for (var i=0; i<links.length; i++) {
    links[i].onclick = function() {
      var query = this.getAttribute("href").split("?")[1];
      var url = "people.php?"+query;
      return !grabFile(url);
    };
  }
}
```

The prepareLinks function needs to be executed as soon as the document has finished loading:

```
window.onload = prepareLinks;
```

From here on, the JavaScript remains much the same as before. The getHTTPObject function is used again. The grabFile function is changed slightly to return a value of true or false:

```
function grabFile(file) {
  var request = getHTTPObject();
  if (request) {
    request.onreadystatechange = function() {
      parseResponse(request);
    };
    request.open("GET", file, true);
    request.send(null);
    return true;
  } else {
    return false;
  }
}
```

The parseResponse function is exactly the same as before:

```
function parseResponse(request) {
  if (request.readyState == 4) {
    if (request.status == 200 || request.status == 304) {
      var details = document.getElementById("details");
      details.innerHTML = request.responseText;
    }
  }
}
```

All I need to do is reference this JavaScript file from the head of my .php file:

```
<script type="text/javascript" src="ajax.js"></script>
```

The Ajax behavior appears to work exactly as before. Clicking on a person's name reveals his contact details without refreshing the whole page. But behind the scenes, everything is working very differently.

To start, the markup is a lot cleaner. There are no more inline event handlers. This makes it easier to maintain the content, and easier to maintain the JavaScript.

The biggest difference is in the way JavaScript is being used. It is enhancing the existing functionality instead of trying to be the sole provider of that functionality. If JavaScript is disabled, everything still works, albeit with page refreshes.

FORMS

Links aren't the only means of sending data to a server. Forms provide the best way of sending large amounts of information from a browser.

Many Web sites have a contact form, like the one shown in Figure 5.5. This is an easy way of allowing visitors to give their feedback.

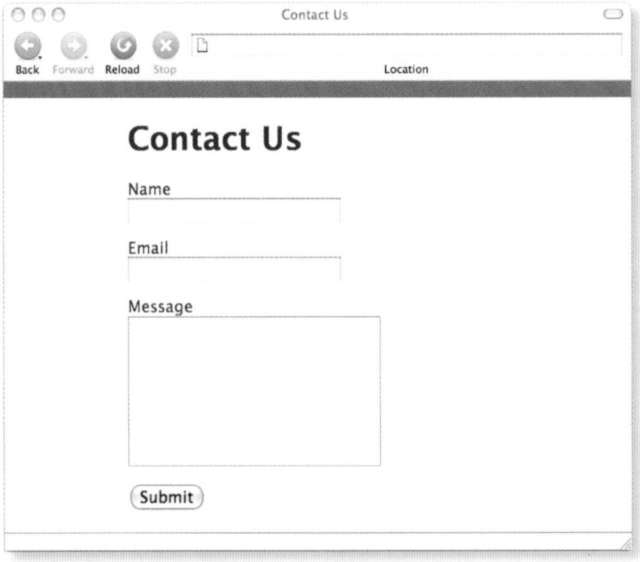

Figure 5.5 A typical form on a contact page.

Here's the source of the contact page:

```
<!DOCTYPE html PUBLIC "-//W3C//DTD XHTML 1.0 Strict//EN"
"http://www.w3.org/TR/xhtml1/DTD/xhtml1-strict.dtd">
<html xmlns="http://www.w3.org/1999/xhtml" xml:lang="en"
lang="en">
<head>
  <meta http-equiv="content-type" content="text/html;
charset=utf-8" />
  <title>Contact Us</title>
  <style type="text/css">
  @import url("style.css");
  </style>
</head>
<body>
  <h1>Contact Us</h1>
  <div id="container">
<?php include "formlogic.php"; ?>
  </div>
</body>
</html>
```

In this case, PHP is being used to create the form inside a `div` called "container."

The `formlogic.php` file carries out a number of tasks:

- If the form has been submitted, check that all the required fields have been filled out.

- If all the required fields have been filled out, display a "thank you" message.

- If a required field hasn't been filled out, display the form and highlight the required field.

- If the form hasn't been submitted at all, display the form.

This is fairly standard form-processing logic. It could be written in any number of server-side programming languages. The end result is that once the processing is done, some markup is output for inclusion in the Web page.

The markup for the form looks like this:

```
<form method="post" id="contactform" action="">
  <p>
    <label for="name">Name</label>
    <input type="text" name="name" id="name" value="" />
  </p>
  <p>
    <label for="email">Email</label>
    <input type="text" name="email" id="email" value="" />
  </p>
  <p>
    <label for="message">Message</label>
    <textarea name="message" id="message" cols="30"
     rows="10">
    </textarea>
  </p>
  <p>
    <input type="submit" name="submit" value="Submit" />
  </p>
</form>
```

In this case, all three fields are mandatory. If the form is submitted and one of the fields has not been filled out, that field is highlighted with some extra text in its `label` element:

```
<label for="name">Name
  <strong class="error">is required</strong>
</label>
```

Once all the required fields have been filled out, the form is no longer displayed. Instead, this message is output:

```
<p class="feedback">
Thank you for getting in touch
</p>
```

At this point, the data that has been submitted via the form can be sent in an email to the Web site owner. The data could also be stored in a database or logged to a file.

CAPTURING FORM DATA

As it stands, the contact form works without any JavaScript. The server handles all of the processing. The only slight irritation is that there's a round trip to the server every time the form is submitted. If a required field hasn't been filled out, the user won't find out until the entire page, with the updated form, comes back from the server. Getting rid of these page refreshes would enhance the user's experience.

I'm going to use some Ajax to send the form data straight to the `formlogic.php` file. To do this, I'll write a function called `sendData`. This function works a lot like the `grabFile` function you've seen already. The function takes a single argument, which is the string of data that will be sent to the server:

```
function sendData(data) {
  var request = getHTTPObject();
  if (request) {
    request.onreadystatechange = function() {
      parseResponse(request);
    };
    request.open( "POST", "formlogic.php", true );
    request.setRequestHeader("Content-Type",
      "application/x-www-form-urlencoded");
    request.send(data);
    return true;
  } else {
    return false;
  }
}
```

This time, the request to the server is using the POST method, not GET:

```
request.open( "POST", "formlogic.php", true );
```

Because data is being sent, it's important to set the content-type header correctly using `setRequestHeader`:

```
request.setRequestHeader("Content-Type",
"application/x-www-form-urlencoded");
```

The `sendData` function returns a Boolean value. If it is successful, the function returns a value of `true`. If, on the other hand, an Ajax request can't be initiated, `sendData` returns a value of `false`.

To use this function, I need to pass it some data. I'm going to extract this data from the form when it is submitted. I can do this using the `onsubmit` event handler.

I'm going to write a function called `prepareForm`, which will execute when the document loads:

```
window.onload = prepareForm;
```

Because I don't want to assume anything about the browser's capabilities or the contents of the current document, I have this function begin by doing some object detection:

```
function prepareForm() {
  if(!document.getElementById) {
    return;
  }
  if(!document.getElementById("contactform")) {
    return;
  }
```

Now I can assign an anonymous function to the form's `onsubmit` event handler:

```
document.getElementById("contactform").onsubmit = function()
{
```

To extract the data from the form, I can make use of a handy shortcut. The `elements` array contains all the form elements in a specified form. Looping through this single array is a lot easier than using the DOM to find all of the form's `input` elements, `textarea` elements, and `select` elements:

```
var data = "";
for (var i=0; i<this.elements.length; i++) {
  data+= this.elements[i].name;
  data+= "=";
  data+= escape(this.elements[i].value);
  data+= "&";
}
```

The variable `data` begins as an empty string. As I loop through the form elements, the name of each element (`name`, `email`, `message`, and so on) is added to this string. Then, an equals sign is appended. After that, the value of the form element is added. I'm making use of JavaScript's escape function to ensure that the value is correctly formatted for its journey to the server. Finally, an ampersand is added to separate the name/value pairs.

At the end of the loop, the variable data holds a string of names and values. This is what I want to pass to the sendData function.

Once again, I will return a Boolean value. This is the opposite of the value returned by sendData:

```
return !sendData(data);
```

If sendData works correctly and it returns a value of true, this statement returns a value of false. The default browser behavior will be canceled. The form won't be submitted.

Here's the finished function:

```
function prepareForm() {
  if(!document.getElementById) {
    return;
  }
  if(!document.getElementById("contactform")) {
    return;
  }
  document.getElementById("contactform").onsubmit =
function() {
    var data = "";
    for (var i=0; i<this.elements.length; i++) {
      data+= this.elements[i].name;
      data+= "=";
      data+= escape(this.elements[i].value);
      data+= "&";
    }
    return !sendData(data);
  };
}
```

When the form is submitted, its data is extracted and passed to the sendData function. The sendData function then sends this data to the formlogic.php file. The server sends back a response, which I need to handle in the parseResponse function:

```
function parseResponse(request) {
  if (request.readyState == 4) {
    if (request.status == 200 || request.status == 304) {
      var container = document.getElementById("container");
      container.innerHTML = request.responseText;
      prepareForm();
    }
  }
}
```

The responseText property returned from the server is inserted into the "container" div by updating its innerHTML property. Then the prepareForm function is executed once more. If the server returns the form with error messages, I'll need to hijack its submit event again.

These functions, prepareForm, sendData, and parseResponse, are all placed in a file called ajax.js, along with the getHTTPObject function. All I need to do is reference this JavaScript file from a <script> tag in the Web page:

```
<script type="text/javascript" src="ajax.js"></script>
```

Now the form processing will take place without any full-page refreshes, as shown in Figure 5.6.

Figure 5.6 Required fields are flagged without a whole page refresh.

Form validation

Using JavaScript to avoid page refreshes when processing a form is nothing new. Form validation is one of the oldest uses of JavaScript. But it has always suffered from an enormous drawback: unreliability.

You cannot rely on JavaScript alone to validate data submitted in a form. JavaScript might be unsupported in the user's browser, or simply switched off. Whatever form validation is carried out in the browser with JavaScript must be repeated in another programming language once the information reaches the server. This means duplicating your logic, which is never a good idea.

The Hijax approach avoids this duplication. JavaScript is used solely as a transport mechanism, sending data to the server and displaying the subsequent response.

If I want to make the processing of my contact form smarter, I just need to update my formlogic.php file. I could add a regular expression that tests whether the `email` value looks like a proper email address. Perhaps I might decide that the `name` field isn't mandatory after all. These are all decisions about the processing logic. It's much better that this processing takes place only on the server. With each new decision, I only have to update one file. Because the JavaScript file isn't attempting to do anything too clever, it isn't affected by changes in the business logic.

This also keeps the size of the JavaScript file to a minimum. A very complex form might require a lot of intricate validation. All of this can be handled on the server, where file size isn't an issue. Even as the form increases in complexity, the JavaScript remains simple.

For the end user, this is all academic. The end result is a snappy response in the browser without a page refresh.

The Deceptively Rich Client

Traditionally, the Web browser has played a subservient role to the Web server. The server can process information, extract dynamic data from a database, and send the resulting page to the browser. The browser is simply the vessel for retrieving and displaying these pages. In this relationship, the browser is what's known as a thin client. The server is where the thick of the action takes place.

With the advent of JavaScript, the capabilities of the browser were enhanced. It was now possible to create richer, more dynamic interaction directly in the browser. But, as we've seen, the presence of JavaScript cannot be taken for granted. If JavaScript is used in an unobtrusive way, enhancements can be added to improve the user experience without breaking the fundamental client-server model. Fundamentally, the browser is still a thin client.

Some Ajax applications have shifted the balance of power. By harnessing the power of JavaScript and the DOM, these applications use the browser to carry out complex programming tasks that are integral to the application's operation. I believe this is a mistake.

Before Ajax, a Web site worked like a self-service restaurant. Every time you wanted some information, the browser had to fetch a new page. In a self-service restaurant, whenever you want some food, you have to go up to the counter to order it.

Adding Ajax to a Web site is like hiring a waiter for a restaurant. The customer no longer needs to go to the counter to order food. The waiter will take the order to the counter instead. This results in a much more pleasant dining experience.

Just because you've hired a waiter doesn't mean you can fire the cook. Yet this is exactly what some Ajax applications attempt to do. Not content with having a waiter take orders and bring food, they get the waiter to do all the cooking too.

Cooking should happen in the kitchen. Application logic belongs on the server. It's better for everyone that way. Your application will work more consistently when it is server-based. The browser environment is simply too unpredictable.

Your users are interested in one thing. They want a pleasant experience when they're using your site. That is where the strength of Ajax really lies. Ajax allows you to create responsive, interactive interfaces. When used correctly, Ajax can be a charming and attentive waiter.

From the user's perspective, the browser now seems to be a rich client. Rich clients, like desktop applications, carry out processing instructions immediately, in situ. A Web site that has been enhanced using the Hijax methodology appears to do the same. Forms are processed and links are fetched, all without a browser refresh. The action appears to be taking place within the browser. In fact, all of the heavy lifting is still being done on the server, where it belongs.

Hijax is deceptive. It creates the illusion that the browser is a rich client when, in fact, this is a facade. Don't feel bad about deceiving your users this way. To borrow from James Carville, "It's the user experience, stupid." That's what really matters.

Summary

When progressive enhancement meets Ajax, the result is Hijax. In my experience, it's a simple but powerful way of applying Ajax. It allows you to update part of a page instead of the whole page, which is the very essence of Ajax interaction. Most importantly, Hijax enhancements can be stripped away without changing the fundamental functionality of your pages. Your Web site's business logic remains bulletproof.

The examples you've seen in this chapter have been simple and straightforward. They could be greatly improved with the addition of some interactive pizzazz. In the next chapter, we'll be looking at ways of providing more feedback for your users.

I also want to examine some important issues. Ajax can be a useful tool, but sometimes it introduces as many problems as it solves. Developing with Ajax raises a number of unique challenges. I'll show you how to confront them.

6

Ajax Challenges

Dodging Bullets

Ajax allows you to explore new forms of interaction. Instead of being tied to the page-based model of requests and responses, you are now free to add more discrete, focused interactivity to your Web sites. This is exciting, but it is also potentially dangerous.

Change can be scary. While it is tempting to sweep away everything that has come before and replace it with shiny new Ajax-powered interfaces, this would be a mistake. Your users would not thank you for it. It is unrealistic to expect people to feel instantly comfortable in a brave new Web.

Users have expectations that are built upon conventions. Ajax breaks some of those conventions. That means that Ajax messes with user expectations, which is rarely a wise move.

If we're not careful, the convention-busting, expectation-breaking nature of Ajax will scare users away. If their initial experience of a new Ajax interface is uncomfortable, they may never come back. If, on the other hand, the transition to Ajax is handled in a careful and respectful manner, the new enhancements will seem obvious, useful, and pleasing.

With all the hype surrounding Ajax, it sometimes sounds like a magic bullet. While there's no doubt that Ajax can bring enormous benefits, it also introduces many design challenges. If these challenges aren't dealt with deftly, you might end up using the magic bullet to shoot yourself in the foot.

Backward Compatibility

Technologies like Ajax can be used to enhance the user experience. But that doesn't mean the technology should be a requirement.

CSS and JavaScript do not have to be present for users to access content. If these technologies are not applied in a thoughtful manner, they can be a dreadful impediment. But as long as the principle of progressive enhancement drives your workflow, the end result will always be backward compatible. This is especially important for Ajax-powered Web pages.

As you've seen, the Hijax approach lets you implement Ajax as an enhancement rather than a requirement. With enough planning and consideration, no user is left behind. As with any methodology, there is an unavoidable question: Does it scale?

All of the examples you've seen so far have been relatively simple. The user interaction driving the contact details page or the feedback form was as straightforward as clicking a link or filling out a form. There's nothing new about that. The Web is built around links and forms: GET and POST. What's changed is the way that these requests are handled. Thanks to Ajax, the browser seems like a rich client, displaying responses within a page without refreshing the whole page. Because traditional links and forms trigger the Ajax functionality, it's not hard to ensure that a fallback solution is always available.

The examples I've given thus far have been traditional Web sites enhanced with Ajax so that they become slightly more application-like. But the term *Ajax* also refers to applications that just happen to be on the Web.

Ajax is a broad term. It covers everything from snappy forms right up to word processors and email clients. There is a sliding scale with straightforward Web pages at one end and fully blown in-browser chat clients at the other. The challenge of providing backward compatibility increases as you move along this scale.

DOCUMENTS AND APPLICATIONS

In discussions about the difference between Web sites and Web applications, you'll often hear about how the Web seems to be in a state of transition. It appears to be moving from a document-delivery platform to an application-based system. But this is a disingenuous distinction; it implies that applications aren't centered on documents.

In fact, documents are at the heart of applications as well as Web sites. A word processor is useless without a document. A spreadsheet application requires a spreadsheet. Even a complex desktop application like Adobe Photoshop works on documents; the documents just happen to be images.

The difference between Web sites and Web applications lies in how malleable a document is. A traditional Web site simply displays a document. A Web application lets you interact with—and change—that document. But make no mistake: the World Wide Web is based on documents, no matter how interactive they become.

That said, as one moves along the sliding scale from Web site to Web application, it becomes more difficult to offer a rich interactive experience that can also degrade gracefully to a series of simple HTML documents.

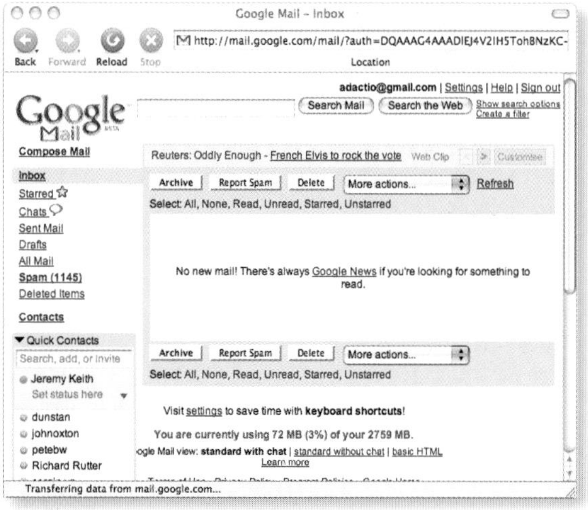

Figure 6.1 Gmail is Google's online email client, enhanced with Ajax.

The continuum

An online email client like Google's Gmail is enhanced through the use of Ajax (https://mail. google.com/). Updating discrete parts of the page improves the user experience. But online email clients can also be made using full-page refreshes, so it is theoretically possible to build an Ajax email client that also degrades gracefully.

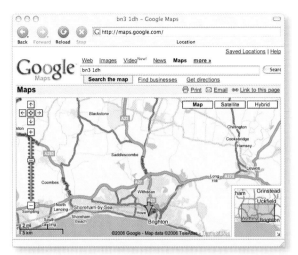

Figure 6.2 Google Maps uses Ajax to create an entirely new way of navigating maps.

Figure 6.3 Meebo is a chat client delivered through a Web browser.

Google Maps is a revolutionary way of interacting with maps because of the JavaScript that powers it (http://maps.google.com/). The ability to drag the visible map area, combined with the Ajax functionality that loads images as needed, creates a very rich interface. It's hard to imagine how this functionality might degrade gracefully without an unacceptable number of page refreshes.

Meebo is a chat client built entirely inside the Web browser using markup, CSS, and JavaScript (http://meebo.com/). Thanks to Ajax, you can chat in virtual windows just as you would in a desktop application. This is a very impressive achievement. It may well be impossible to provide this kind of interaction without using Ajax.

Hijax will take you surprisingly far along the sliding scale from Web page to Web application. But, at some point, the goal of backward compatibility may simply become unachievable.

If you find yourself at this point, it may come as a relief. Finally, you are freed from worrying about providing graceful degradation. But be careful what you wish for. Either you will need to build a separate non-Ajax version of your site, or you will have to turn users away. Neither option is particularly appealing.

The numbers game

You may be able to justify the decision to make an exclusive application if you believe you know your audience from tracking browser statistics. Statistics can be misleading, however. The decision not to support a particular Web browser may be based on circular reasoning: the statistics show very few visits from some browser, therefore there's no point supporting it—but the reason there are so few visits is that the site doesn't support that browser.

It's important to remember that you aren't building Web sites for numbers, percentages, or even browsers. Web sites are used by people. Your statistics may show that 97 percent of your visitors are using Ajax-capable browsers. The remaining 3 percent of your total traffic sounds like a small amount. But if your site has 500 visitors a day, that figure translates to 15 people who are being turned away each day. Every person visiting your site should have access to its content.

I'm not suggesting that each and every visitor to your site should have exactly the same experience. That's the great thing about progressive enhancement: it lets you provide each visitor with as much or as little functionality as they can handle, while ensuring that everyone has access to the content. If you decide to make Ajax a requirement, you will miss out on the key benefits of using Web standards like HTML/XHTML, CSS, and JavaScript. Should you decide to forego the benefits of progressive enhancement, you may be better off using a different technology.

If you use the Flex framework and deliver your Web application in Flash, you can provide a very rich interface in a stable, predictable environment: the Flash player. Of course, the Flash player plug-in will be a requirement for the user to access the application. But if you have already decided that you are going to exclude visitors on technological grounds, you are simply swapping one group of excluded users for another.

Use the right tool for the job at hand. The biggest advantage of Ajax over Flex is that Ajax can be applied as an enhancement, whereas the Flash player offers all-or-nothing content delivery. If you decide not to avail your site of Ajax's greatest strength, you should certainly explore other options for providing rich interactivity on your Web sites.

Web Services

As described in Chapter 3, the open method of the XMLHttpRequest object can only make requests to the same domain as itself. This is an infuriating stumbling block if you want to retrieve data from a third-party service.

Many applications allow access to their data through public Application Programming Interfaces, or APIs. APIs usually return data in XML, which would appear to make them ideally suited to Ajax requests. However, the same-domain restriction prevents this union.

If a Web service provides an option to supply data formatted as JSON, the script tag hack can be used to retrieve that data. The problem with this solution is that it requires JavaScript in order to work. There is no non-JavaScript fallback.

A more robust solution involves the use of a proxy. A proxy is simply a gateway that relays requests. Using your own server as a proxy for third-party services, you can make Ajax requests as usual. The XMLHttpRequest object requests a file on your own server. This file then sends a request to the Web service on a third-party server, which returns some data. This data can be passed back to the XMLHttpRequest object.

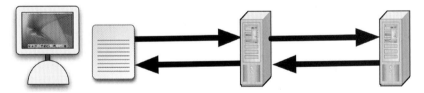
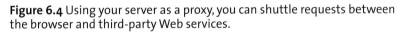

Figure 6.4 Using your server as a proxy, you can shuttle requests between the browser and third-party Web services.

The downside to using a proxy is that the requests and responses must pass through an extra gateway. This extra hop means that the data won't flow quite as quickly as it would without a proxy.

The great advantage to using a proxy is that JavaScript is not a requirement. You can build a Web site that uses full-page requests to retrieve data from a Web service and then use Hijax to add the Ajax interactivity. If Ajax is not supported, the data is still available through traditional full-page interaction.

If you use your server as a proxy for communicating with Web services, it makes sense to parse the data on your server rather than use JavaScript. It's a lot faster to convert XML into HTML on your server than in a browser.

Feedback

Web browsers are built around the traditional, page-based model of content delivery. By default, when a link is clicked or a form is submitted, the browser sends a request to a server for a new page. At this point, the browser instantly provides feedback to let the user know that something is happening.

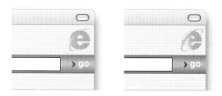

Figure 6.5 The logo for Microsoft's Internet Explorer begins spinning the moment a new page is requested.

In most Web browsers, this feedback takes the form of some kind of animation. Apple's Safari shows an expanding strip of color in the background of the address bar. In Microsoft's Internet Explorer, the normally static logo in the corner begins to spin when the user requests a new page.

With Ajax, the default browser behavior of fetching a whole new page is replaced with custom actions written using JavaScript and event handlers. Because the usual behavior is canceled, the browser no longer indicates that some action is under way. It's up to us to provide that feedback.

In an ideal world, Ajax responses would be received instantaneously. In reality, a resource requested via Ajax is subject to the same bottlenecks as any other traffic on the Internet. The speed of the response is determined by bandwidth, latency, and all the other factors that govern the flow of data on a network.

For a visitor to an Ajax-enabled Web page, this could be potentially disorienting. If clicking a link or submitting a form produces no immediate response, the logical assumption is that something is broken.

To deal with this issue, Ajax scripts should include some mechanism to indicate that an action is under way. You could use DOM Scripting to insert a piece of explanatory text into the page. This might be as simple as writing the text "Loading…" into an appropriate element.

A more effective solution would be to use animation. Take a leaf out of the browser manufacturer's book. Create an endlessly looping animated image and then display this image until the response is successfully received.

The simplest format for this kind of image is an animated GIF file. The exact image can be anything you like, as long as it features a smoothly looping animation. Rotating shapes, spinning arrows, and barbershop-pole progress bars are all popular conventions for indicating activity.

Figure 6.6 Some of the possible ways to show activity.

Here's a short function called displayLoading. It takes a single argument, which is an element in the document. This element is first emptied by removing all of its child nodes. Then, a newly created img element is appended.

```
function displayLoading(element) {
  while (element.hasChildNodes()) {
    element.removeChild(element.lastChild);
  }
  var image = document.createElement("img");
  image.setAttribute("src","loading.gif");
  image.setAttribute("alt","Loading...");
  element.appendChild(image);
}
```

Now I can update the contact details example to use this function. I want to execute it at the same time that I'm starting the Ajax request in the grabFile function:

```
function grabFile(file) {
  var request = getHTTPObject();
  if (request) {
    displayLoading(document.getElementById("details"));
    request.onreadystatechange = function() {
      parseResponse(request);
    };
    request.open("GET", file, true);
    request.send(null);
    return true;
  } else {
    return false;
  }
}
```

When a name is clicked, a GIF animation appears in the "details" div, which is where that person's details will appear.

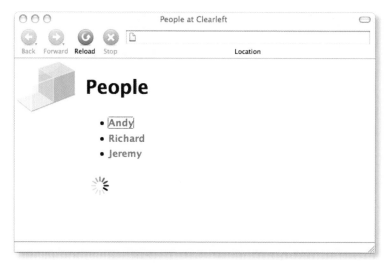

Figure 6.7 A spinning icon reassures visitors that something is happening.

Once the Ajax call is successfully completed, the loading image is obliterated by the use of `innerHTML` in the `parseResponse` function:

```
function parseResponse(request) {
  if (request.readyState == 4) {
    if (request.status == 200 || request.status == 304) {
      var details = document.getElementById("details");
      details.innerHTML = request.responseText;
    }
  }
}
```

For the contact form, I want to display a GIF animation at the bottom of the form when it's submitted. I'm going to amend the `displayLoading` function so that it doesn't empty the containing element before appending the image. This time I'm using a progress bar:

```
function displayLoading(element) {
  var image = document.createElement("img");
  image.setAttribute("src","progressbar.gif");
  image.setAttribute("alt","Loading...");
  element.appendChild(image);
}
```

I just need to update the sendData function:

```
function sendData(data) {
  var request = getHTTPObject();
  if (request) {
    displayLoading(document.getElementById("contactform"));
    request.onreadystatechange = function() {
      parseResponse(request);
    };
    request.open( "POST", "formlogic.php", true );
    request.setRequestHeader("Content-Type",
      "application/x-www-form-urlencoded");
    request.send(data);
    return true;
  } else {
    return false;
  }
}
```

Now a progress bar will appear as soon as the form is submitted.

Figure 6.8 A progress bar below the contact form shows that an action is under way.

WHAT JUST HAPPENED?

Just as it is important to show that something is happening, it's also a good idea to show that something just happened.

In 37signals' suite of Ajax applications, the company pioneered the yellow fade technique (www.37signals.com). Using a combination of JavaScript and CSS, a Web page displays an updated element with a yellow background color that gradually fades to white. This is an effective way of showing which part of the current page has changed.

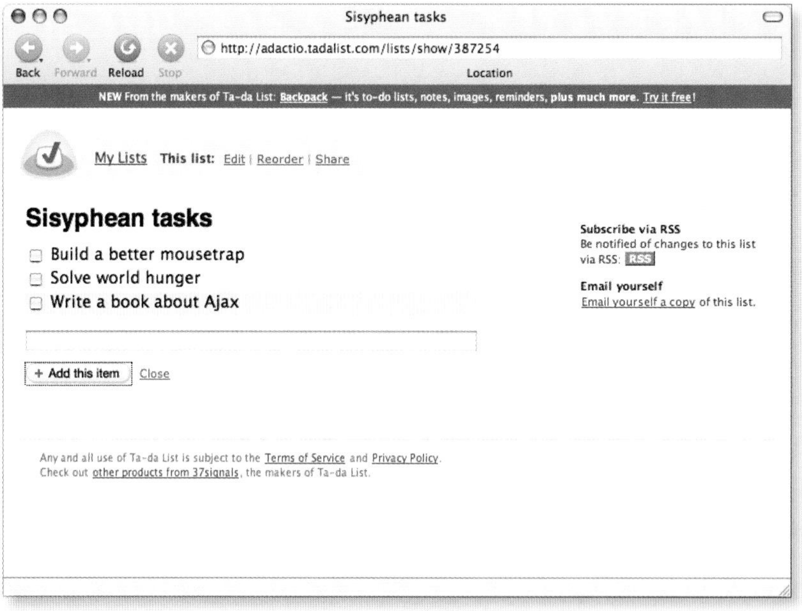

Figure 6.9 The yellow fade technique in action.

The yellow fade technique has been employed on quite a few sites—so much so that it is now a convention of sorts. This is good. Users find repeated conventions reassuring. The more a visual feedback technique is used, the clearer its meaning becomes.

Here's a function that fades an element's background color to white:

```
function fadeUp(element,red,green,blue) {
  if (element.fade) {
    clearTimeout(element.fade);
  }
  element.style.backgroundColor = "rgb("+red+","+green+",
    "+blue+")";
  if (red == 255 && green == 255 && blue == 255) {
    return;
  }
  var newred = red + Math.ceil((255 - red)/10);
  var newgreen = green + Math.ceil((255 - green)/10);
  var newblue = blue + Math.ceil((255 - blue)/10);
  var repeat = function() {
    fadeUp(element,newred,newgreen,newblue)
  };
  element.fade = setTimeout(repeat,100);
}
```

The `fadeUp` function takes four arguments. The first argument is the element that will have its background color altered. The other three arguments are RGB values: red, green, and blue. These are the starting RGB values of the element's background color:

```
function fadeUp(element,red,green,blue)
```

The `backgroundColor` of the element's `style` property is updated with the red, green, and blue values. With CSS, you can declare color values using hexadecimal or RGB values:

```
element.style.backgroundColor = "rgb("+red+","+green+",
  "+blue+")";
```

This is a recursive function, meaning it calls itself. There is a slight pause before the function calls itself again. This pause is achieved using `setTimeout`, which takes two arguments: the function to be executed and the number of milliseconds to wait before executing it:

```
var repeat = function() {
  fadeUp(element,newred,newgreen,newblue)
};
element.fade = setTimeout(repeat,100);
```

In this case, I'm attaching the time-out to a custom property of the element called `fade`. Every time the function is called, the time-out is flushed using `clearTimeout`. This ensures that there won't be any conflicting instructions if the `fadeUp` function is ever applied to the same element more than once at the same time:

```
if (element.fade) {
  clearTimeout(element.fade);
}
```

Before the function is called again, the RGB values are increased to bring each of them closer to 255:

```
var newred = red + Math.ceil((255 - red)/10);
var newgreen = green + Math.ceil((255 - green)/10);
var newblue = blue + Math.ceil((255 - blue)/10);
```

When each of the values reaches 255, the element's background color is white: `rgb(255,255,255)`. The function no longer needs to repeat:

```
if (red == 255 && green == 255 && blue == 255) {
  return;
}
```

The `fadeUp` function allows me to add a yellow fade, or any other colored fade, as long as the background color of my document is white.

I can add a yellow fade to the contact details page by updating the `parseResponse` function:

```
function parseResponse(request) {
  if (request.readyState == 4) {
    if (request.status == 200 || request.status == 304) {
      var details = document.getElementById("details");
      details.innerHTML = request.responseText;
      fadeUp(details,255,255,153);
    }
  }
}
```

I'm starting with a shade of yellow that has a value of `rgb(255,255,153)`. When the Ajax response is returned, this color will fade to white.

Figure 6.10 Adding a subtle fade indicates which part of the page has been updated.

I'm using yellow because users may find it familiar from other Ajax applications. In other situations, the fading color could be used for added context. For contact forms, you could use a shade of red to draw attention to any errors.

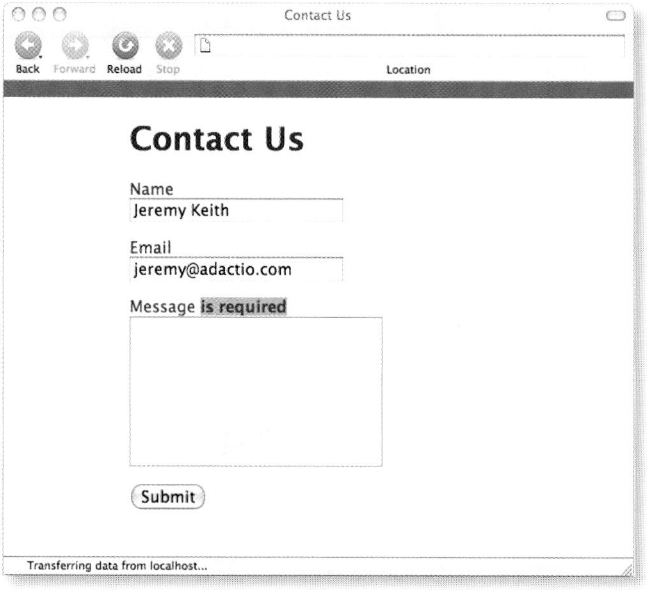

Figure 6.11 A pale red fade indicates a problem area.

The fadeUp function I've written is quite basic and works only on documents with a white background. For a more robust script, check out the Fade Anything Technique (www.axentric.com/aside/fat/).

Browser Behavior

The lack of a spinning icon isn't the only difference that Ajax brings to a browser's behavior. Many of the tools and shortcuts that are built into Web browsers are based on the traditional model of full-page refreshes.

BOOKMARKING

Almost every Web browser includes functionality for storing bookmarks. The architecture of the World Wide Web is built around the idea of uniquely identified resources. These resources are usually pages, and their unique identifiers are URLs. If you can store the value of a page's URL, you can instantly jump to that page without following a link from another page. Bookmarks (or "favorites") are simply URLs that a browser stores at your request so that you can return to the associated pages at a later date.

When an Ajax action takes place, the URL is not updated. The contents of the current document may have changed, but there's no way for you to bookmark the document in its changed state.

Take the contact details page, for example. I can bookmark this page only in its initial state. Through the power of Ajax, Richard Rutter's contact details can be displayed on the same page without a full-page refresh. If I try to bookmark the page while these contact details are visible, I will still bookmark the page only in its original state. The URL does not change. As far as the browser is concerned, this is the same page.

This poses quite a challenge. We are doing away with full-page refreshes, but at the same time we want to update the current URL. We want to have our cake and eat it too.

This isn't a new problem. In Chapter 1, I made the tongue-in-cheek observation that a frameset is a form of Ajax. As it turns out, frames suffered from this same problem. No matter how deep inside a frameset you navigated, the URL in the address bar of your browser remained constant.

The only way to bookmark a page that is contained within a frameset is to right-click and open the frame in a new browser window. Hijax allows for a similar workaround. I can right-click Richard Rutter's name and open that link in a new window.

It's nice that Hijax offers links that you can bookmark, but right-clicking to spawn a new window isn't an intuitive action for most users. Bookmarking a link has changed from something straightforward to something laborious.

THE BACK BUTTON

Another challenge, one that is closely related to the bookmarking issue, lies with the browser's back button.

Bookmarks are links that users add at will. The browser doesn't bookmark every page you visit; you must actively add a page to your bookmark list. Your Web browser creates a different list to keep track of all the pages you have recently visited. These URLs are automatically stored in the browser's history.

The back button and forward button let you navigate quickly backward and forward through the pages you recently visited. The back button in particular has become an indispensable tool for the average user. If you follow a link to a page but then wish you hadn't, the back button allows you to turn back the clock and return to the previous page. It is the Web browser's equivalent of the "undo" action in desktop applications.

When part of a page is changed using Ajax, the browser's history does not get updated. As far as the browser is concerned, the URL hasn't changed; therefore, the user has not moved forward. At this point, the back button is no longer the useful tool it once was. Clicking the back button will take the user further back than they may wish. It certainly won't act like an undo mechanism.

Again, this isn't an entirely new problem. For many years, Flash movies were divorced from the history stack. No matter how deeply you navigated through a Flash movie, the browser's back button would take you back to the page before the movie rather than stepping back through the movie itself. Some Flash developers attempted to solve this problem by removing the back button from the browsing experience. Pages with Flash movies were opened in new browser windows with all the browser chrome removed. This was a draconian solution. The back button is far too valuable, both practically and psychologically, to take away from your users.

Solutions

Many smart Ajax developers have attempted to tackle the twin challenges of bookmarking and the back button. Most of the solutions involve the addition of an internal anchor to the current URL, as well as some trickery with a hidden `iframe` (see the article "Ajax: How to Handle Bookmarks and Back Buttons," by Brad Neuberg, at http://onjava.com/lpt/a/6293).

These solutions, while clever, are inevitably convoluted. They need to be, in order to deal with the inconsistent behavior exhibited by different browsers (see the article "Fixing the Back Button and Enabling Bookmarking for Ajax Apps," by Mike Stenhouse, at www.contentwithstyle.co.uk/Articles/38/).

It would be better if the situation could be avoided in the first place.

If you are updating so much of the page that your users believe they have moved to a new page, you are probably doing too much. If Ajax is used to alter small, discrete portions of a document, then it is unlikely that any problems will arise with bookmarking or using the back button.

When you are deciding whether to replace full page refreshes with Ajax requests, ask yourself, Would I want to bookmark the changed state of this page? If the answer could be yes, then you should probably decide against using Ajax.

This isn't always an easy question to answer. Sometimes the answer varies from person to person. Think about a search form: should the results be displayed without using a page refresh? It may seem like a usability enhancement, but someone may want to bookmark the search results, or at least the first page of the results. After the first page of search results, you may decide to use Ajax for paginating deeper into the results. If the search results take up a significant portion of the page, you'll need to update a large chunk of the document. That's probably not a good idea. Your users may feel that they are actually moving between pages and would rightly expect to be able to navigate using the back button as well.

The cognitive dissonance surrounding the back button isn't entirely new to Ajax. The back button has never really meant "undo" in all browsing situations. If I fill out and submit a form, my data is sent to the server and I am directed to a new page. Clicking the back button won't undo the act of sending that information.

Judicious use of Ajax should ensure that problems with the back button and bookmarking never arise to begin with. When in doubt, do some user testing. Actually, even if you have no doubts, you should still do some user testing. However, you may find that trying to do user testing with Ajax applications introduces its own problems.

Wireframing

Most Web sites don't start life as pixels. Before a line of markup is written, a plan is usually in place. Through the discipline of information architecture, you can formulate and fine-tune the structure of a Web site as well as individual Web pages. This kind of structural planning is often crafted using wireframes, which are documents that outline the infrastructure of a site or page.

Because wireframes are cheaper and easier to produce than finished Web pages, they can provide enormous savings by highlighting potential problems early in the site-building process. Even some rudimentary user testing with wireframes printed on paper can result in beneficial feedback.

The traditional model of the Web maps very well onto paper prototypes: a single wireframe represents a single Web page. Once Ajax enters the equation, that balance is upset. How is it possible to test multiple interactions within a single document?

As Jeffrey Zeldman so succinctly put it, "Wireframing Ajax is a bitch" (www.alistapart.com/articles/web3pointo/).

I don't have any easy solutions to this problem. It may be that the usefulness of wireframing is negated by the complexity of Ajax. It's certainly hard to imagine how Ajax interaction could be tested so early in the development process.

There seems to be little choice but to develop a bare-bones prototype early on for testing. This prototype need not be fully functional as long as it can simulate the effects of Ajax. The effects might be as simple as hiding and showing portions of the document based on the user's actions. This could be achieved using some straightforward DOM Scripting, without the need for full-blown Ajax requests. Nonetheless, even the simplest functional prototype will require more time and effort than a simple wireframe.

THE ARROW OF TIME

Until now, wireframes were good enough at describing how a Web page should be structured. Until now, Photoshop comps were good enough at describing how a Web page should look. Neither technique is well suited to describing how a Web page should behave.

Wireframes and Photoshop comps are static models. They don't change state. Ajax-enhanced Web documents are dynamic. The state of the document can change over time, usually based on the actions of the user. There doesn't seem to be an easy way to represent changes over time in a static document.

Summary

In this chapter, I've tried to highlight some of the common pitfalls in Ajax development. By far the greatest challenge is providing functionality to user-agents that don't support Ajax. Even once this is dealt with, there are many other issues to overcome. The solutions to most of these problems can be found by empathizing with the user in the following ways:

- Provide reassuring feedback as soon as an Ajax request is initiated.

- Indicate clearly which part of the current document has been updated.

- Don't alter the state of the document so much that it would upset the expected behavior of the back button.

- If users will want to bookmark the altered state of a document, don't use Ajax.

Following these guidelines will keep your Ajax applications from becoming overly confusing.

There is a bigger challenge that I haven't mentioned until now. In the next chapter, we will tackle a very thorny issue: can Ajax be accessible?

7

Ajax and Accessibility

Doing the Right Thing

In an oft-quoted remark, Sir Tim Berners-Lee said:

"The power of the Web is in its universality. Access by everyone regardless of disability is an essential aspect."

The first sentence refers to the power of universal access. Using the principle of progressive enhancement, you can harness that power pretty easily. If you build your Web sites on a foundation of semantic, well-structured markup and then use technologies like CSS and JavaScript to add extra layers of presentation and behavior, you can rest assured that your content will be accessible by any user-agent.

As you've seen, the same approach can be taken with Ajax. The Hijax technique lets you add snazzy interactivity for the benefit of modern browsers, while ensuring that older browsers can still access the same content and functionality.

Sir Tim's second sentence is a little more problematic. On the Web, just as in the real world, there is a moral imperative not to discriminate based on disability.

As long as the text is legible and the images are clear, a Web page's information should be accessible. Visually impaired users require some help to gain access to the same information. Assistive technology can provide that help. People with weak vision often employ screen-magnifying software to increase the size of text and images. People with very serious visual impairment, such as blindness, are more likely to use screen-reading software.

Understanding Screen Readers

A screen reader is a piece of software that converts visual information on a computer into a nonvisual output such as speech or Braille. The term is something of a misnomer: many screen-reader users don't have screens connected to their computers.

Apple's Mac OS X operating system features a built-in screen reader called VoiceOver. This is still in its infancy and isn't being used much yet. The majority of screen readers are commercial products designed to work with Windows operating systems. These include SuperNova and Hal from Dolphin Computer Access, Window-Eyes from GW Micro, and JAWS from Freedom Scientific.

These screen readers sit between the operating system and the user. The software attempts to make sense of the output being delivered by whatever program is currently in use. In order to access Web pages with a screen reader, blind users must still use a Web browser such as Firefox or, more commonly, Internet Explorer.

SCREEN READERS AND WEB BROWSERS

Most screen readers don't interact directly with the DOM structure of a Web page. Instead, the software takes a snapshot of the document when the page loads. This content is then placed into a virtual buffer. Without this virtual buffer, screen readers would only be able to interact with forms and links—

elements that can receive focus from input devices. Thanks to the virtual buffer, screen-reader users can navigate their way through other elements like headers, images, and tables.

Most screen readers share some common characteristics, such as being able to toggle between modes of interaction. JAWS, for instance, can toggle between a virtual PC cursor mode (making use of the virtual buffer) and a PC cursor mode that interacts directly with focusable elements in a Web page. JAWS also offers a forms mode, but this behaves identically to the PC cursor mode as form elements can take focus. Window-Eyes has a browse mode that uses its virtual buffer. When the browse mode is disabled, the screen reader can interact directly with focusable elements. So, roughly speaking, the browse mode in Window-Eyes corresponds to the virtual PC cursor mode in JAWS.

SCREEN READERS AND JAVASCRIPT

There is a common misconception that screen readers aren't capable of executing JavaScript. In fact, the underlying Web browser determines the JavaScript capability. However, screen readers do behave erratically in response to JavaScript events.

For example, if JAWS is in virtual PC cursor mode, it reacts to the `onclick` event handler and refreshes its virtual buffer. Other event handlers don't fare quite so well. The `onreadystatechange` event handler, which lies at the heart of Ajax requests, does not trigger a refresh. It's a similar story for Window-Eyes in browse mode.

Screen Readers and Ajax

If screen readers don't automatically respond to Ajax updates, how can we design Ajax-enhanced Web sites so that they inform screen-reader users when something has changed? That's the fundamental problem with Ajax and assistive technology.

It's easy to show sighted users when part of a page has been updated. The yellow fade technique is one way of indicating not only that content has been inserted or changed, but also exactly where the change occurred. Providing a similar feedback mechanism for screen readers is a huge challenge.

Screen readers show a bias toward certain elements. For example, screen readers can access form fields and links directly because they can take focus. Tables are also treated as special cases because they can have such complicated structures making it difficult for blind people to navigate them. If an Ajax request results in creating or updating these kinds of elements, there's a greater likelihood that the screen reader will notice the generated content. In practice, most Ajax requests generate content within ordinary elements such as `div` elements.

GIVING FOCUS

One way of harnessing the inherent bias of screen readers is to update the tab order of the page. This is the order in which focusable elements like links and form fields can be accessed. Each focusable element has a tab index that is usually assigned automatically, but that can also be assigned through the `tabindex` attribute. Messing around with the default tab order of a document is a bad idea, however. Web pages that are well structured already have a logical tab order.

There is a somewhat hackish trick that lets you make an element focusable without upsetting the existing tab order. The `tabindex` attribute is supposed to contain a positive value ranging from zero to 32,767. Despite this, many browsers let you specify a negative `tabindex` value. In these browsers, a `tabindex` value of minus one allows an element to accept focus without interfering with the tab order of the document.

Here's a typical function triggered by the `onreadystatechange` event handler. The `responseText` property is placed inside a `div` called `"details"` using `innerHTML`:

```
function parseResponse(request) {
  if (request.readyState == 4) {
    if (request.status == 200 || request.status == 304) {
      var details = document.getElementById("details");
      details.innerHTML = request.responseText;
    }
  }
}
```

Once the "details" div is updated, give it a tabindex value of minus one. Then, the div can be focused using JavaScript:

```
function parseResponse(request) {
  if (request.readyState == 4) {
    if (request.status == 200 || request.status == 304) {
      var details = document.getElementById("details");
      details.innerHTML = request.responseText;
      details.tabindex = -1;
      details.focus();
    }
  }
}
```

This technique doesn't work in all browsers. Safari ignores the negative tabindex value. If a screen reader like JAWS or Window-Eyes is in a mode that uses the virtual buffer, the element will be focused but its content won't be read automatically. The user needs to request manually that the virtual buffer be refreshed before the content can be read. If the screen reader is in a mode that doesn't use the virtual buffer, the user doesn't have to do anything in order to hear the new content.

For more information on how different devices react to this technique, read the results of testing done by Steve Faulkner and Gez Lemon (http://juicystudio.com/article/making-ajax-work-with-screen-readers.php).

ALERTING

The tabindex hack doesn't work in all situations. There are many possible permutations of a screen reader's make, version, and mode, not to mention all the possible variations of the underlying browser.

An alternative approach is to use an alert dialog to inform the user that part of the page has changed. These dialogs are part of the operating system, so there's a greater chance a screen reader will notice them.

The biggest disadvantage of using alert dialogs is that they are intrusive and annoying. They should almost certainly be an opt-in extra.

You could, for instance, begin your document with a check box and some text that asks the user if he or she wishes to be notified of Ajax updates:

```
<p class="opt-in-question">
<label>
Would you like to be informed of changes made to the page
by JavaScript?
<input type="checkbox" id="alert-opt-in" />
</label>
</p>
```

Using an external CSS file, this message can be hidden from sighted users. Don't make the mistake of using display: none; that will hide the message from screen readers too. Instead, try shunting the message off the screen:

```
.opt-in-question {
  position: absolute;
  left: -999px;
  width: 990px;
}
```

Now the parseResponse function can be updated to find out if the check box is checked or not. If it is checked, an alert dialog is displayed:

```
function parseResponse(request) {
  if (request.readyState == 4) {
    if (request.status == 200 || request.status == 304) {
      var details = document.getElementById("details");
      details.innerHTML = request.responseText;
      var box = document.getElementById("alert-opt-in");
      if (box.checked) {
        alert ("The page has been updated.");
      }
    }
  }
}
```

As long as the check box is checked, an alert dialog pops up every time the page is updated.

This technique isn't very helpful. It's nice that screen-reader users can be informed that a document has been updated, but they then have to manually trigger a refreshed reading of the entire document. This can be extremely frustrating. In many ways, it would be better for screen-reader users if they could bypass the Ajax functionality entirely.

> **note**
>
> Hiding form elements introduces new problems. The hidden form element is included in the document's tab index. This is confusing for users who navigate using a keyboard. People with motor impairments may not be able to use a mouse, relying on keyboard navigation instead. Hiding a form off-screen in an attempt to help one group of disabled users—the visually disabled—will cause problems for a different group.

Figure 7.1 An alert dialog is displayed whenever the page is updated.

State of the Art

The current level of support for Ajax in screen readers leaves a lot to be desired. Clearly, Web browsers have evolved at a faster rate than assistive technology.

James Edwards, the JavaScript expert better known by his moniker Brothercake, tested the current crop of screen readers to find out how they deal with generated content (http://www.sitepoint.com/article/ajax-screen-readers-work).

The results are not encouraging. Brothercake sums up his findings:

"I'm forced to conclude that, unless a way can be found to notify screen readers of updated content, Ajax techniques cannot be considered accessible, and should not be used on a production site without a truly equivalent non-script alternative being offered to users up-front."

At the same time that Brothercake released the results of his test cases, another accessibility expert published some Ajax-related material. Joe Clark, author of *Building Accessible Websites*, conducted a series of tests on the Basecamp application from 37signals. He presented the results at the Iceweb conference in 2006 (http://joeclark.org/access/research/ice/iceweb2006-test-results.html).

Joe's conclusions aren't quite as pessimistic as Brothercake's:

"What we can say, then, is that this Ajax application is usable by screen-reader users some of the time. They aren't totally shut out, but it isn't totally easy for them, either."

Nonetheless, the results make it clear that the presence of Ajax in the application is an annoying hindrance for screen-reader users.

A MODEST PROPOSAL

Derek Featherstone is an expert in JavaScript, accessibility, and the intersection of the two (http://boxofchocolates.ca/).

At the @media conference in London in 2005, Derek expressed his frustration with screen-reader technology's handling of generated content. As he pointed out, we can deal with user-agents that support JavaScript and we can deal with user-agents that don't support JavaScript, but we have a much harder time dealing with user-agents like screen readers that support only a subset of JavaScript functionality. In a daring move, Derek suggested that we should encourage users of outdated screen-reader technology to switch JavaScript off. After all, if we are building our Ajax applications using progressive enhancement, then everything will degrade gracefully.

In practice, it isn't so easy to simply disable JavaScript in the browser. Even for a sighted user, it can be hard to find the right check box in a browser's preferences. In Internet Explorer, for example, the control for JavaScript is found in Internet Options under Security, where it is called Active Scripting.

Nonetheless, Derek's point is well taken. If Ajax is proving to be more of a hindrance than a help for screen-reader users, non-Ajax interaction is preferable. It would be better if screen readers didn't initiate Ajax requests only to fail at a critical point later on.

BYPASSING AJAX

The hidden check box can be repurposed for bypassing Ajax functionality:

```
<p class="opt-in-question">
<label>
This page uses Ajax functionality which may cause problems
for screen readers. Would you like to disable this
functionality?
<input type="checkbox" id="disable-opt-in" />
</label>
</p>
```

Instead of waiting until the Ajax request is complete, you can test the state of this check box before initiating the request in the first place:

```
function grabFile(file) {
  var box = document.getElementById("disable-opt-in");
  if (box.checked) {
    return false;
  }
  var request = getHTTPObject();
  if (request) {
    request.onreadystatechange = function() {
      parseResponse(request);
    };
    request.open("GET", file, true);
```

```
    request.send(null);
    return true;
  } else {
    return false;
  }
}
```

In order to save the user from having to check the box every time, you could store a value in a cookie, using either JavaScript or your server-side language of choice. Even then, this is a fairly clunky solution.

Google's Gmail application contains text that, theoretically, is only displayed to screen readers. The text reads, "If you are using a screen reader, you may wish to switch to basic HTML for a better experience." The text contains a link to the non-Ajax version of the application.

Figure 7.2 Hidden text in Google's Gmail application.

This is a thoughtful addition, but it requires the existence of a "separate but equal" non-Ajax site. Building parallel applications is rarely desirable. Ideally, one single site should be able to adapt to the needs of its visitors.

DETECTING SCREEN READERS

Using hidden text and check boxes requires a lot of participation on the part of the screen-reader user. The mere presence of an outdated screen reader should be enough to trigger a bypass of Ajax functionality.

There is no way to directly detect the presence of a screen reader using JavaScript. It is possible to glean plenty of information about the Web browser accessing the current document, but, because screen readers work on top of the browser, their presence goes unannounced.

While Web browsers can't detect or communicate the presence of screen readers, other applications can. The current Flash player, for instance, can detect a screen reader's make and whether it is currently enabled. By itself, this capability of the Flash plug-in doesn't appear to help us much.

Flash has made huge strides in functionality and power in recent years. One of the many innovations introduced to the Flash player is a Flash-JavaScript bridge. It is now possible to trigger a JavaScript function from within a Flash movie. Combined with Flash's screen-reader detection, this opens up some possibilities for bypassing Ajax.

FlashAid

FlashAid is a proof-of-concept application written by Aral Balkan (http://osflash.org/flashaid).

A small, 1-pixel-by-1-pixel movie checks for the presence of a screen reader and passes the result to a JavaScript function. This function can then act on the result accordingly. For instance, a global variable could be given a Boolean value of `true` or `false`, depending on the result returned by the Flash movie. Based on the value of this variable, Ajax requests can then be executed or bypassed.

FlashAid is still in its infancy and requires plenty of testing. It would be useful to find out just what percentage of screen-reader users have a recent version of the Flash player plugged into their browsers.

A mailing list has been set up to take the research and development of FlashAid further (http://osflash.org/mailman/listinfo/flashaid_osflash.org).

The Future

Current screen readers don't seem to be able to deal with Ajax applications effectively. Or, to take a different perspective, it's fair to say that current browsers aren't able to effectively communicate changes of state in a way that's meaningful to assistive technology.

This situation will change.

In XHTML 2, there are plans for embedding role and state values that can be used to declare explicitly how an element should behave. This behavioral information can then be read directly by screen readers.

Here's an example from the W3C Web site of an element that acts as an interactive slider widget:

```
<span id="slider" class="myslider myselector2"
role="wairole:slider"
waistate:valuemin="0"
waistate:valuemax="50"
waistate:valuenow="33">
</span>
```

A "Roadmap for Accessible Rich Internet Applications" has already been published by the W3C (http://www.w3.org/TR/aria-roadmap/).

These additions will undoubtedly make life better for users of assistive technology as long as browser makers and screen-reader manufacturers follow the specifications.

For the time being, we are stuck with outdated technology. Ajax is pushing the boundaries of technology on the Web. Browsers have reached an acceptable level of support, but screen readers are lagging behind.

THE INNOVATOR'S DILEMMA

Web developers today are faced with a difficult decision. Ajax can be used to provide significant usability enhancements. Yet, wherever Ajax is implemented, there's a good chance that it will negatively affect accessibility.

When confronted with this tough choice, it seems that the morally acceptable solution is to forgo Ajax entirely. Yet this would mean deliberately avoiding technological improvements that would benefit the majority of users.

At the same time, the needs of screen-reader users can't simply be ignored. If there were a straightforward way of making Ajax applications accessible, the problem would merely be one of implementation. As it is, there are no easy answers.

It is slightly unfair that Web developers are asked to shoulder so much responsibility. There is also an onus on screen-reader manufacturers to update their products to keep pace with the latest developments.

Summary

On the face of it, the situation with Ajax and accessibility looks grim. Although there are some clever hacks that might help screen readers access generated content, there is no way to make the Ajax experience as seamless as it is for sighted users.

Still, these are early days. There may well be accessibility solutions just waiting to be discovered. Further testing by users of screen readers on real-world Ajax applications may reveal unexpected opportunities for increased accessibility.

The Web development community is very fortunate to have smart, talented people like Brothercake, Derek Featherstone, Joe Clark, and others tackling this issue.

8

Putting It All Together

Building a Better Bookshop

So far you've learned about these key areas:

- The code required for Ajax interaction

- The principle of progressive enhancement

- Design challenges posed by Ajax

In this chapter, I put all of that theory to the test. It's time to build an Ajax application.

I'm using PHP to create this application, but you can use any server-side language. Don't worry if you don't understand PHP. Understanding the language I'm using isn't as important as following the underlying concepts.

You can download the source code for this chapter at http://bulletproofajax.com/shop/files/.

Planning

I'm building an online bookshop called Bulletproof Books. You can find a working version at http://bulletproofajax.com/shop/

The target audience of this shop is the discerning Web developer, so only the finest books on Web development will be stocked. It won't be a very large store; in fact, the site consists of just one page.

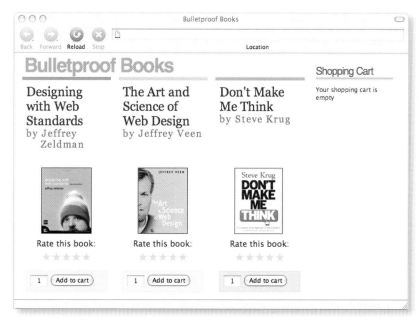

Figure 8.1 Bulletproof Books will stock a small but essential range of books.

The main purpose of the site is to allow visitors to add books to a shopping cart. In this utopian example, none of the books have prices, but obviously that wouldn't be the case with a real e-commerce site.

The functionality isn't limited to shopping. Visitors can also rate books on a scale from one to five.

Before I start coding all this interaction, I need to think about the underlying structure of the page.

STRUCTURE

The page begins with some straightforward branding: the name of the shop. Then, the page is divided into two parts. The first division holds all the available products. This is the main content. The second division holds the shopping cart.

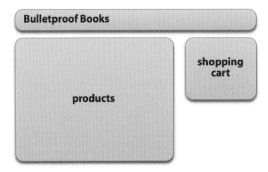

Figure 8.2 The broad structure of the page.

The XHTML structure looks like this:

```
<!DOCTYPE html PUBLIC "-//W3C//DTD XHTML 1.0 Strict//EN"
"http://www.w3.org/TR/xhtml1/DTD/xhtml1-strict.dtd">
<html xmlns="http://www.w3.org/1999/xhtml" xml:lang="en"
lang="en">
 <head>
  <meta http-equiv="content-type" content="text/html;
charset=utf-8" />
  <title>Bulletproof Books</title>
 </head>
 <body>
  <h1>Bulletproof Books</h1>
   <div id="mainContent">
   </div>
   <div id="subContent">
    <h2>Shopping Cart</h2>
    <div id="basket">
    </div>
   </div>
 </body>
</html>
```

I'm using the div element to divide the markup into sections. These divisions are reflected in the file structure on the server. A series of files are combined on the server to serve up a complete document.

This is the structure of the framework page, index.php:

```
<h1>Bulletproof Books</h1>
<div id="mainContent">
<?php include "products.php"; ?>
</div>
<div id="subContent">
<h2>Shopping Cart</h2>
<div id="basket">
<?php include "shoppingcart.php"; ?>
</div>
</div>
```

The include statements in index.php pull in two files: products.php and shoppingcart.php.

The products.php file assembles the markup for the products. In a real application, the product data would probably be stored in a database. For this example, I'm simply storing the data in a PHP array:

```
<?php
$products = array(
 1 => array(
  "id" => "zeldman",
  "cover" => "zeldman.jpg",
  "title" => "Designing with Web Standards",
  "author" => "Jeffrey Zeldman"
 ),
 2 => array(
  "id" => "veen",
  "cover" => "veen.jpg",
  "title" => "The Art and Science of Web Design",
  "author" => "Jeffrey Veen"
 ),
 3 => array(
  "id" => "krug",
  "cover" => "krug.jpg",
```

```
  "title" => "Don't Make Me Think",
  "author" => "Steve Krug"
 )
);
```

Looping through this array, I then create a `div` for each product:

```
foreach ($products as $product) {
 echo '
<div class="product" id="'.$product["id"].'">
 <dl class="info">
  <dt>'.$product["title"].'</dt>
  <dd>by '.$product["author"].'</dd>
 </dl>
 <img class="cover" src="images/'.$product["cover"].'"
   alt="'.$product["title"].'" />
 <div class="rating">';
 $id = $product["id"];
 include "rating.php";
 echo '
 </div>
 <form class="shopping" method="post" action="index.php">
  <fieldset>
   <input type="text" class="amount" name="amount"
     value="1" />
   <input type="hidden" name="product"
     value="'.$product["title"].'" />
   <input type="submit" name="action" value="Add to cart" />
  </fieldset>
 </form>
</div>
';
}
?>
```

In each loop, I'm creating a variable called `$id` and then including a file called rating.php. This file creates a list for each item. The list contains five links that can be used to rate the product.

Here's an example of the markup produced by products.php and rating.php:

```
<div class="product" id="zeldman">
 <dl class="info">
  <dt>Designing with Web Standards</dt>
  <dd>by Jeffrey Zeldman</dd>
 </dl>
 <img class="cover" src="images/zeldman.jpg"
  alt="Designing with Web Standards" />
 <div class="rating">
  <p>Rate this book:</p>
  <ul>
   <li><a class="worst" title="hate it"
     href="?product=zeldman&amp;rating=worst">1</a></li>
   <li><a class="bad" title="don't like it"
     href="?product=zeldman&amp;rating=bad">2</a></li>
   <li><a class="fair" title="it's fine"
     href="?product=zeldman&amp;rating=fair">3</a></li>
   <li><a class="good" title="like it"
     href="?product=zeldman&amp;rating=good">4</a></li>
   <li><a class="best" title="love it"
     href="?product=zeldman&amp;rating=best">5</a></li>
  </ul>
 </div>
 <form class="shopping" method="post" action="index.php">
  <fieldset>
   <input type="text" class="amount" name="amount"
     value="1" />
   <input type="hidden" name="product"
     value="Designing with Web Standards" />
   <input type="submit" name="action"
value="Add to cart" />
  </fieldset>
 </form>
</div>
```

The markup displays some basic information about the product, followed by an image. Then it displays the ratings list. Finally, it shows a form for adding this product to the shopping cart. This same structure is applied to all the products.

Figure 8.3 The structure of a single product.

FUNCTIONALITY

As well as displaying the list of numbers for rating a product, the rating.php file contains the functionality for storing the rating for the current product:

```
if (isset($_GET['product']) && $_GET['product'] == $id) {
 if (isset($_GET['rating'])) {
  $_SESSION[$id] = $_GET['rating'];
 }
}
```

Again, don't worry if you don't understand the PHP code: the underlying functionality is the important thing.

If a query string is sent containing a value for *product* and that value matches the current product, and the query string also contains a value for *rating,* that rating value is stored in a session variable. A session variable, usually stored as a cookie, is a quick and easy way of storing the value. In a real application, the value would probably be stored in a database.

In this case, the name of the session variable is the ID of the current product, and the value is the rating that has been sent in the query string.

If a session variable exists for the current product, the markup is updated accordingly:

```
if (isset($_SESSION[$id])) {
 echo '
 <p>Your rating:</p>
  <ul class="'.$_SESSION[$id].'">';
 } else {
 echo '
 <p>Rate this book:</p>
  <ul>';
}
```

If a query string is sent as `product=zeldman&rating=best`, the ratings markup looks like this for the Zeldman product:

```
<p>Your rating:</p>
<ul class="best">
```

The functionality for rating products is now in place. The shopping-cart functionality still needs to be added. That will be handled by the shoppingcart.php file.

Shopping

The shoppingcart.php file pulls in a file called Cart.inc. This is a class that handles all the shopping transactions using methods like getProducts, addProduct, removeProduct, and so on:

```php
<?php
class Cart {
  function countTotal() {
  }
  function getProducts() {
  }
  function addProduct($product) {
  }
  function removeProduct($product) {
  }
  function processInput($data = array()) {
  }
}
?>
```

I won't go into the details of the PHP code involved. All you need to know is that these methods take care of all the functionality required for a shopping cart.

In the shoppingcart.php file, a new instance of this class is created as a session variable (again, if this were a real application, you would probably use a database instead):

```php
if (!isset($_SESSION["cart"])) {
  $_SESSION["cart"] = new Cart();
}
```

If any data has been posted from a form, the Cart class takes care of adding products to the session variable:

```php
if (count($_POST)>0) {
  $_SESSION["cart"] -> processInput($_POST);
}
```

Now, depending on the contents of the session variable, either a short message is displayed or a table showing the contents of the shopping cart is shown:

```
if ($_SESSION["cart"] -> countTotal() < 1) {
 echo '
 <p>Your shopping cart is empty</p>
 ';
} else {
 echo '
  <table>
   <thead>
    <tr>
     <th>Item</th>
     <th><abbr title="quantity">Qty</abbr></th>
    </tr>
   </thead>
   <tbody>';
 foreach ($_SESSION["cart"] -> getProducts() as
   $product => $count) {
  echo '
    <tr>
     <td>'.stripslashes($product).'</td>
     <td>'.$count.'</td>
    </tr>';
  }
 echo '
  </tbody>
 </table>
 ';
}
```

In this way, the markup for the whole page is output, and information received via query strings and forms is processed.

PRESENTATION

Now that the structure of my application is in place, I can add style information to the document using CSS.

In the head element of the page, I'm adding a link element that points to a CSS file:

```
<link rel="stylesheet" media="screen" type="text/css"
href="styles/basic.css" />
```

This file, basic.css, imports a series of other CSS files:

```
@import url("layout.css");
@import url("ratings.css");
@import url("products.css");
@import url("basket.css");
```

Each of these files takes care of styling a different part of the page.

The layout.css file arranges the div elements on the page:

```
#mainContent {
 width: 77%;
 position: relative;
 float: left;
}
#subContent {
 width: 20%;
 position: relative;
 float: left;
}
```

The file products.css contains the color and font information for the product data. Here's a sample of the CSS:

```
.product {
 border-top: 6px solid #ccc;
 width: 27%;
 min-width: 10em;
 padding: .5em;
 margin: 0 .5em;
 float: left;
}
#zeldman {
 border-top-color: #693;
}
#veen {
 border-top-color: #fc3;
}
#krug {
 border-top-color: #f93;
}
```

The basket.css file contains some basic styling for the shopping-cart table.

Ratings

Figure 8.4 The background image for the ratings.

The file for styling the ratings for each product is ratings.css. This is quite complex. The CSS displays stars for each rating and fills in the appropriate number of stars when you hover over each link. For an in-depth explanation of this technique, see http://komodomedia.com/blog/index. php/2005/08/24/creating-a-star-rater-using-css/.

The text inside the ratings list is replaced with a background image of stars that is 200 pixels wide. The first 100 pixels has filled-in stars. The next 100 pixels has unfilled stars.

```css
.rating ul {
 list-style: none;
 position: relative;
 width: 100px;
 height: 20px;
 background: transparent url("../images/stars.gif")
  -100px 0 no-repeat;
 padding: 0;
 left: 50%;
 margin-left: -50px;
 overflow: hidden;
}
```

If a class has been applied to the list, the background image is positioned accordingly:

```css
.rating ul.worst {
 background-position: -80px 0;
}
.rating ul.bad {
 background-position: -60px 0;
}
.rating ul.fair {
 background-position: -40px 0;
}
.rating ul.good {
 background-position: -20px 0;
}
.rating ul.best {
 background-position: 0 0;
}
```

The text for each link in the list is hidden:

```
.rating li {
  margin: 0;
  padding: 0;
  float: left;
}
.rating li a {
  display: block;
  position: absolute;
  width: 20px;
  height: 20px;
  text-indent: -100px;
  overflow: hidden;
  z-index: 20;
}
```

Each link in the list is postioned differently. As the scale increases, the position is moved farther along:

```
.rating a.worst {
  left: 0;
}
.rating a.bad {
  left: 20px;
}
.rating a.fair {
  left: 40px;
}
.rating a.good {
  left: 60px;
}
.rating a.best {
  left: 80px;
}
```

When the user moves the pointer over any of these links, a repeating background image of a darker-colored star is added:

```
.rating li a:hover {
  background: transparent url("../images/star.gif")
    left top repeat-x;
```

Figure 8.5 As you hover the pointer over each link in the ratings scale, the corresponding number of stars appears.

```
left: 0;
z-index: 1;
}
```

The width of the link increases according to its position in the scale:

```
.rating a.worst:hover {
width: 20px;
}
.rating a.bad:hover {
width: 40px;
}
.rating a.fair:hover {
width: 60px;
}
.rating a.good:hover {
width: 80px;
}
.rating a.best:hover {
width: 100px;
}
```

Applying Ajax

At this stage, Bulletproof Books is functional: you can rate books and add them to your shopping cart. It's fairly useless without a link to a checkout page, but this is just an example, after all.

The application is built in a modular fashion:

■ The products.php file outputs a chunk of XHTML that displays all the products.

■ The rating.php file outputs a snippet of XHTML for a list of ratings for a single product.

■ The shoppingcart.php file outputs the XHTML for a table of products added to the shopping cart.

A familiar Ajax pattern emerges as you look at the functionality handled by some of these individual files:

- **Ratings.** Whenever you click on a ratings link, information is sent to the server in a query string. The server sends back the same page with only one slight difference: the chosen rating is now displayed with the appropriate product. The rating.php file handles this.

- **Shopping.** Whenever you click an Add to Cart button, information is sent to the server through a form submission. The server sends back the same page, this time with the shopping cart updated to reflect the new addition. The shoppingcart.php file takes care of this.

Both situations are good candidates for the Hijax treatment.

REUSABLE JAVASCRIPT

So far, I have written JavaScript code specifically for each example. But all the examples have followed much the same pattern:

1. One part of a page is a **container** for some links or a form.

2. The **data** from this container is captured.

3. This data is sent to a **URL** on the server via XMLHttpRequest.

4. A **loading** function is triggered to let the user know that something is happening.

5. When the Ajax request is done, part of the page is updated. Let's call this the **canvas**.

6. A **callback** function is triggered to let the user know that something has happened.

The specific details vary from case to case, but the process remains the same.

It seems a shame to reinvent the wheel every time I want to add some Ajax functionality. Instead, I'm going to abstract the process to create a reusable chunk of JavaScript code.

I want to bundle up a number of variables and functions into one self-contained block. That sounds like the perfect job for a user-defined object.

Writing an object

If you recall, JavaScript has three kinds of objects:

1. Native objects such as `Math`, `Date`, and `Array` are provided by the language.

2. Host objects such as `window` are provided by the environment in which JavaScript is running.

3. User-defined objects are created by you, the programmer.

Wrapping up a bunch of variables and functions inside an object is a great way of making your code portable.

I'm going to create an object to handle Ajax requests. The name of this object is `Hijax`. Creating an object is just like creating a function:

```
function Hijax() {
}
```

Now I'm declaring all my variables in one place:

```
function Hijax() {
 var container,url,canvas,data,loading,callback,request;
}
```

- `container` is the element on the page that contains the trigger mechanism for the Ajax request: either a form or a collection of links.

- `url` is the path to a file on the server.

- `canvas` is the part of the page that gets updated.

- `data` is either `null` or a string of name/value pairs to be sent to the server.

- `loading` is a function to be triggered when the Ajax request begins.

- `callback` is a function to be triggered when the Ajax request ends.

- `request` is an instance of `XMLHttpRequest`.

Most of these values need to be set from outside the object. To make that possible, I create a series of methods. Remember, a method is simply a function that is tied to an object. I'm using the `this` keyword, which is shorthand for "this current object":

```
function Hijax() {
 var container,url,canvas,data,loading,callback,request;
 this.setContainer = function(value) {
  container = value;
 };
 this.setUrl = function(value) {
  url = value;
 };
 this.setCanvas = function(value) {
  canvas = value;
 };
 this.setLoading = function(value) {
  loading = value;
 };
 this.setCallback = function(value) {
  callback = value;
 };
}
```

Each of these methods can be accessed from outside the object. Suppose I create a new instance of the `Hijax` object, like this:

```
var myobject = new Hijax();
```

I can now access its methods using the dot syntax:

```
myobject.setUrl("rating.php");
```

The presence of the `this` keyword allows the methods to be accessed from outside the object. These methods then take care of assigning values to `container`, `url`, `canvas`, `loading`, and `callback`. The other values, `data` and `request`, are created within the object.

I create one more method that can be accessed from outside the object. This is called `captureData`:

```
this.captureData = function() {
};
```

When this method is triggered, data is extracted from the `container` element.

I begin by testing the `nodeName` property of `container` to see if it is a form:

```
if (container.nodeName.toLowerCase() == "form") {
```

If it is, then I want to extract the values from the form when it is submitted:

```
container.onsubmit = function() {
 var query = "";
 for (var i=0; i<this.elements.length; i++) {
  query+= this.elements[i].name;
   query+= "=";
   query+= escape(this.elements[i].value);
   query+= "&";
   }
```

I have concatenated the names and values of the form elements into a variable called query. Now I'm assigning this value to data:

```
data = query;
```

In that single line, I am making use of one of the most powerful capabilities of JavaScript: closures.

Closures

Normally there are two kinds of variable scope in JavaScript:

1. Global. If a variable is declared outside a function, it can be accessed from anywhere.

2. Local. If a variable is declared within a function using the var keyword, it can be accessed only from within that parent function.

Something interesting happens when a function is nested within another function. The nested function can also access any local variables belonging to the parent function:

```
function test() {
 var foo = "bar";
 function getFoo() {
  alert (foo);
 }
}
```

This is an example of a closure. Normally the getFoo function would have access only to global variables or its own local variables. Because getFoo is nested within the test function, it can also access the local variables of test.

Think of closures as a kind of regional scope: broader than local but not as broad as global.

Thanks to closures, functions within an object can access variables declared within the same object. Remember, a function within an object is a method, and a variable within an object is a property. The captureData method of the Hijax object has access to the data property even though that property was declared outside the method:

```
function Hijax() {
  var container,url,canvas,data,loading,callback,request;
  ...
  this.captureData = function() {
   if (container.nodeName.toLowerCase() == "form") {
    container.onsubmit = function() {
     var query = "";
     for (var i=0; i<this.elements.length; i++) {
      query+= this.elements[i].name;
      query+= "=";
      query+= escape(this.elements[i].value);
      query+= "&";
     }
     data = query;
    };
   }
  };
  ...
}
```

The really remarkable characteristic of this particular closure is the way that scope is maintained even within the onsubmit event handler. Normally it would be impossible to reference anything other than a global variable from within an event-handling function. Thanks to the power of closures, all of the variables declared within an object are still available when an event-handling function is called from within that object.

Once the data from the form has been captured, another method, called start, is invoked. This method initiates the Ajax request. If the start method is successful, it returns a value of true. In that case, I want to cancel the default browser behavior for the submit event:

```
return !start();
```

If the start method returns true, the onsubmit event handler returns the opposite, which is false. If, on the other hand, the start method fails and it returns a value of false, the onsubmit event handler returns the opposite value, `true`, which means the default browser behavior kicks in and the form is submitted as normal.

Before getting to the `start` method, I need to finish writing the `captureData` method.

If the `container` element is not a form, then the data is being transmitted via links instead. By looping through all of the links within the `container` element, I can add an `onclick` event-handling function to capture any data contained in query strings:

```
var links = container.getElementsByTagName("a");
for (var i=0; i<links.length; i++) {
 links[i].onclick = function() {
  var query = this.getAttribute("href").split("?")[1];
  url+= "?"+query;
  return !start();
 };
}
```

In this case, the closure is the `url` property, which is being updated with the link's query string.

The finished `captureData` method looks like this:

```
this.captureData = function() {
 if (container.nodeName.toLowerCase() == "form") {
  container.onsubmit = function() {
   var query = "";
   for (var i=0; i<this.elements.length; i++) {
    query+= this.elements[i].name;
    query+= "=";
    query+= escape(this.elements[i].value);
    query+= "&";
   }
   data = query;
   return !start();
  };
 } else {
  var links = container.getElementsByTagName("a");
  for (var i=0; i<links.length; i++) {
   links[i].onclick = function() {
    var query = this.getAttribute("href").split("?")[1];
```

```
    url+= "?"+query;
    return !start();
  };
 }
 links = null;
 }
};
```

I've included a little bit of housecleaning for Internet Explorer. Versions 5 and 6 of that browser aren't very good at cleaning up references to DOM nodes. The `links` variable is no longer needed once the `captureData` method is finished, but, unlike other browsers, Internet Explorer doesn't perform garbage collection on this variable. Once the `onclick` event handlers have been assigned, the statement `links = null` performs the garbage collection manually.

Initiating the Ajax request

Once data has been intercepted from either a form or a link, the `start` method is executed.

I could create the start method like this:

```
function start() {
}
```

I'm writing it like this instead:

```
var start = function() {
};
```

The two are equivalent, but I prefer to use the second style when I'm writing the methods of an object.

The `start` method is a straightforward function that returns either `true` or `false`:

```
var start = function() {
 request = getHTTPObject();
 if (!request || !url) {
  return false;
 } else {
  initiateRequest();
  return true;
 }
};
```

As long as a URL has been specified for the Ajax request and the function getHTTPObject successfully creates an instance of XMLHttpRequest, the start method returns a value of true.

The getHTTPObject function should be quite familiar to you. Now that it is nested within the Hijax object, getHTTPObject is a method of Hijax:

```
var getHTTPObject = function() {
 var xmlhttp = false;
 if (window.XMLHttpRequest) {
  xmlhttp = new XMLHttpRequest();
 } else if(window.ActiveXObject) {
  try {
   xmlhttp = new ActiveXObject("Msxml2.XMLHTTP");
  } catch (e) {
   try {
    xmlhttp = new ActiveXObject("Microsoft.XMLHTTP");
   } catch (e) {
    xmlhttp = false;
   }
  }
 }
 return xmlhttp;
};
```

In the start method, the result of getHTTPObject is assigned to the request property:

```
request = getHTTPObject();
```

If getHTTPObject returns an instance of XMLHttpRequest, the start method invokes a method called initiateRequest before returning a value of true:

```
initiateRequest();
return true;
```

The initiateRequest method is the engine that drives the Hijax object. First of all, this method tests whether a function has been assigned to the loading property of the current Hijax object. If the loading property has a value, now is the time to execute it:

```
var initiateRequest = function() {
 if (loading) {
  loading();
```

```
  }
};
```

The `initiateRequest` method contains the three building blocks of
`XMLHttpRequest`: `onreadystatechange`, `open`, and `send`.

A reference to a method called `completeRequest` is assigned to the
`onreadystatechange` event handler:

```
request.onreadystatechange = completeRequest;
```

If data has been captured from a form, a `POST` request is specified in the
`open` method and the `data` property is passed to the server in the `send`
method:

```
request.open("POST", url, true);
request.setRequestHeader("Content-Type",
  "application/x-www-form-urlencoded");
request.send(data);
```

If `data` has no value, a `GET` request is specified and no data is sent to the
server:

```
request.open("GET", url, true);
request.send(null);
```

Determining which kind of request to initiate is accomplished with a
straightforward `if` statement that tests the value of `data`. The finished
`initiateRequest` method looks like this:

```
var initiateRequest = function() {
  if (loading) {
    loading();
  }
  request.onreadystatechange = completeRequest;
  if (data) {
    request.open("POST", url, true);
    request.setRequestHeader("Content-Type",
      "application/x-www-form-urlencoded");
    request.send(data);
  } else {
    request.open("GET", url, true);
    request.send(null);
  }
};
```

Once the Ajax request is initiated, all that remains is to handle the response from the server.

Completing the Ajax request

A method called `completeRequest` has been attached to the `onreadystatechange` event handler. As usual, there is a test to see if the `readyState` property has reached 4 and if the server is sending a `status` of 200 or 304:

```
var completeRequest = function() {
 if (request.readyState == 4) {
   if (request.status == 200 || request.status == 304) {
```

If the `canvas` property of the current `Hijax` object has been specified, that part of the page is updated with the contents of `responseText`:

```
if (canvas) {
 canvas.innerHTML = request.responseText;
}
```

If a function has been assigned to the `callback` property of the current `Hijax` object, that function is executed:

```
if (callback) {
 callback();
}
```

That's all there is to the `completeRequest` method:

```
var completeRequest = function() {
 if (request.readyState == 4) {
   if (request.status == 200 || request.status == 304) {
    if (canvas) {
     canvas.innerHTML = request.responseText;
    }
    if (callback) {
     callback();
    }
   }
  }
};
```

PREPARING THE PAGE

The Hijax object provides a nice reusable way of adding Ajax functionality to a Web page. All the examples in this book so far could be reengineered to use Hijax because they all follow the same steps.

In the case of Bulletproof Books, rating books and adding them to the shopping cart both follow the classic Ajax pattern: user interaction through a form or a link updates a discrete part of the same page.

Each book has an associated list of ratings links as well as a form for adding that product to the shopping cart. There are three books altogether, making a total of six page elements to be given the Hijax treatment. Rather than specifying the details of each Ajax request in turn, I'm creating a function called bookshop to wrap up all the instructions:

```
function bookshop() {
}
```

Within bookshop, I have a method called prepareCart, which will be executed three times, once for each book. This method takes a single argument, which is the form element that will be intercepted:

```
var prepareCart = function(element) {
};
```

I'm creating a new instance of the Hijax object:

```
var xhr = new Hijax();
```

Using the setContainer method, I'm specifying the form element as the container property. This is passed in the element argument:

```
xhr.setContainer(element);
```

The URL for this Ajax request is shoppingcart.php:

```
xhr.setUrl("shoppingcart.php");
```

The part of the page that will be updated is the shopping cart, which has the ID basket. This element is the canvas:

```
xhr.setCanvas(document.getElementById("basket"));
```

Within bookshop, I create a method called displayLoading, which will show a progress bar. In this case, I want the progress bar to appear in the shopping cart:

```
xhr.setLoading(function() {
  displayLoading(document.getElementById("basket"));
});
```

Finally, when the Ajax request is complete, I want to add a yellow fade to the shopping cart. This will be accomplished using a method called `fadeUp`. Fading up the shopping cart like this is the `callback` function:

```
xhr.setCallback(function() {
  fadeUp(document.getElementById("basket"),255,255,204);
});
```

With all of these properties specified, it's time to apply the `captureData` method:

```
xhr.captureData();
```

Now I have a method, `prepareCart`, that I can use to intercept the data from the forms associated with each product.

To intercept the data from each book's ratings links, I have a similar method called `prepareRating`:

```
var prepareRating = function(element) {
  var xhr = new Hijax();
  xhr.setContainer(element);
  xhr.setUrl("rating.php");
  xhr.setCanvas(element);
  xhr.setLoading(function() {
    displayLoading(element);
  });
  xhr.setCallback(function() {
    fadeUp(element,255,255,204);
    prepareRating(element);
  });
  xhr.captureData();
};
```

In this case, the URL is rating.php and the `container` element and `canvas` element are one and the same.

Before I can start passing values to `prepareCart` and `prepareRating`, I need to define the `loading` and `callback` functions, which I specified as `displayLoading` and `fadeUp`, respectively.

What is happening?

The displayLoading function looks like this:

```
var displayLoading = function(element) {
 var image = document.createElement("img");
 image.setAttribute("alt","loading...");
 image.setAttribute("src","images/progressbar.gif");
 image.className = "loading";
 element.appendChild(image);
};
```

This creates a new img element with progressbar.gif as its src. This newly created image is then inserted into the specified page element.

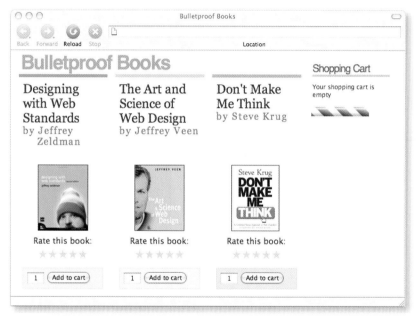

Figure 8.6 A GIF animation indicates that something is happening.

What just happened?

The fadeUp method should be familiar to you from previous examples:

```
var fadeUp = function(element,red,green,blue) {
 if (element.fade) {
```

```
  clearTimeout(element.fade);
}
element.style.backgroundColor = "rgb("+red+","+green+",
  "+blue+")";
if (red == 255 && green == 255 && blue == 255) {
  return;
  }
var newred = red + Math.ceil((255 - red)/10);
var newgreen = green + Math.ceil((255 - green)/10);
var newblue = blue + Math.ceil((255 - blue)/10);
var repeat = function() {
  fadeUp(element,newred,newgreen,newblue)
};
element.fade = setTimeout(repeat,100);
};
```

This changes the background color of a specified page element from the color set in RGB values up to RGB (255, 255, 255), which is white.

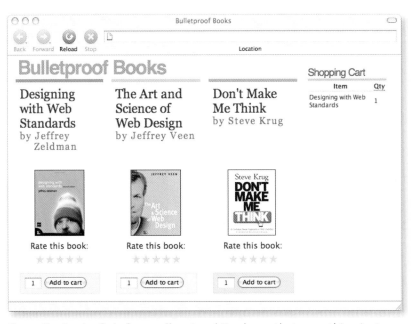

Figure 8.7 A color fade from yellow to white shows that something just happened.

Execution

With all the methods of bookshop in place, I can now assign the right Ajax functionality to the right page elements.

Each book has an associated form that has a class name of shopping. I'm passing each of them to the prepareCart method:

```
var all_forms = document.getElementsByTagName("form");
for (var i=0; i<all_forms.length; i++) {
 if (all_forms[i].className.match("shopping")) {
  prepareCart(all_forms[i]);
 }
}
```

For the sake of older versions of Internet Explorer, I'm cleaning up the all_ forms variable once I'm done with it:

```
all_forms = null;
```

For the rating functionality, I'm passing any div with a class name of rating to the prepareRating method:

```
var all_divs = document.getElementsByTagName("div");
for (var i=0; i<all_divs.length; i++) {
 if (all_divs[i].className.match("rating")) {
  prepareRating(all_divs[i]);
 }
}
all_divs = null;
```

The bookshop function is ready. All I need to do now is execute it. I can't execute it right away, though; I have to wait until the document has loaded:
```
window.onload = bookshop;
```

Better yet, I can use the addLoadEvent function I showed you in Chapter 5:
```
addLoadEvent(bookshop);
```

Bulletproofing

Bulletproof Books is now working. See for yourself at http://bulletproofajax. com/shop/

Everything is working fine, but there's always room for improvement. I'd like to point out a few areas where you might want to tweak the code.

ERROR HANDLING

The `completeRequest` method of the `Hijax` object expects the server to send a `status` property of 200 or 304. If any other status is sent from the server, nothing happens. It's quite easy to build in some kind of error handling to let the user know that the request failed:

```
var completeRequest = function() {
 if (request.readyState == 4) {
  if (request.status == 200 || request.status == 304) {
   if (canvas) {
    canvas.innerHTML = request.responseText;
   }
   if (callback) {
    callback();
   }
  } else {
   alert("Error: "+request.status);
  }
 }
};
```

An `alert` statement isn't the nicest way to display an error message. You could append the error message to the `canvas` element instead.

A more robust solution would allow the error handling to change on a case-by-case basis. Try declaring a new variable in the `Hijax` object called `errorhandler`:

```
var container,url,canvas,data,loading,callback,request,
errorhandler;
```

Create a corresponding method for assigning a function to this property from outside the object:

```
this.setErrorhandler = function(value) {
 errorhandler = value;
};
```

If a function has been assigned to errorhandler, it is executed in the completeRequest method:

```
var completeRequest = function() {
 if (request.readyState == 4) {
  if (request.status == 200 || request.status == 304) {
   if (canvas) {
    canvas.innerHTML = request.responseText;
   }
   if (callback) {
    callback();
   }
  } else {
   if (errorhandler) {
    errorhandler();
   }
  }
 }
};
```

You can now add a method to bookshop to take care of any unexpected errors:

```
var displayError = function(element) {
 var para = document.createElement("p");
 para.className = "error";
 var message = document.createTextNode("Oops! Something went
   wrong.");
 para.appendChild(message);
 element.appendChild(para);
 fadeUp(para,204,51,102);
};
```

Assign this method in prepareCart and prepareRating:

```
xhr.setErrorhandler(function() {
 displayError(element.parentNode);
});
```

You probably want to use a more meaningful error message. You can update the displayError method so that it accepts a second argument—a string of text:

```
var displayError = function(element,errortext) {
 var para = document.createElement("p");
 para.className = "error";
 var message = document.createTextNode(errortext);
 para.appendChild(message);
 element.appendChild(para);
 fadeUp(para,204,51,102);
};
```

Now you can tailor the error message according to the expected Ajax interaction.

TIMING OUT

In an ideal World Wide Web, connectivity would be fast and seamless. In reality, that isn't always the case. Sometimes connections drop, either because of a problem on the server or because of the user's Internet connection.

Ajax requests don't time out automatically. Once a request is initiated, it remains open until the readyState property reaches 4.

The XMLHttpRequest object has an abort method that cancels the Ajax request. Using a setTimeout statement, you can invoke this method if the request is taking too long.

Add a new variable called timer to the Hijax object:

```
var container,url,canvas,data,loading,callback,request,
errorhandler,timer;
```

In the initiateRequest method, assign timer a setTimeout statement:

```
var initiateRequest = function() {
 timer = setTimeout(function() {
  request.abort();
 }, 60000);
```

This aborts the Ajax request after 60 seconds. If an `errorhandler` function has been provided, you might want to invoke that here:

```
timer = setTimeout(function() {
  request.abort();
  if (errorhandler) {
    errorhandler();
  }
}, 60000);
```

Some browsers exhibit the strange behavior of firing the `readystatechange` event when `abort` is invoked. To counteract this, assign an empty function to `onreadystatechange` before aborting the Ajax request:

```
timer = setTimeout(function() {
  request.onreadystatechange = function() {
  };
  request.abort();
  if (errorhandler) {
    errorhandler();
  }
}, 60000);
```

Now you have a way of handling unsuccessful requests. If the request works as planned, you'll need to cancel the `timer` countdown in the `completeRequest` method:

```
var completeRequest = function() {
  if (request.readyState == 4) {
    if (request.status == 200 || request.status == 304) {
      clearTimeout(timer);
```

ACCESSIBILITY

As it stands, the `Hijax` object doesn't make any concessions to screen-reader users but, as we saw in the last chapter, there is no way of consistently informing a screen reader that part of the page has been updated.

You could use the `tabindex` hack to focus the `canvas` area in the `completeRequest` method:

```
var completeRequest = function() {
 if (request.readyState == 4) {
  if (request.status == 200 || request.status == 304) {
   clearTimeout(timer);
   if (canvas) {
    canvas.innerHTML = request.responseText;
    canvas.tabindex = -1;
    canvas.focus();
   }
```

Remember, this doesn't work in every combination of screen reader and Web browser. Also, it may be overkill: do you really want to call the user's attention to the shopping cart every time she adds a new product? Perhaps she would rather continue browsing from her current position in the document.

Summary

Bulletproof Books is a good example of how Ajax can be used to enhance an existing application—an online shop, in this case. The application works just fine without Ajax, but the shopping experience is smoother once Ajax is added to the mix.

The `Hijax` object is a flexible collection of common Ajax patterns. You can use it for more than shopping carts and ratings. Don't treat this object as a finished solution for your Ajax needs. Instead, treat it as a starting point.

In this chapter, I've highlighted just some of the ways that the `Hijax` object could be improved. I'm sure the code can be further refined. There's no such thing as the perfect script. Writing Ajax should be a continuous process of assessment and iteration.

There may not be such a thing as truly bulletproof Ajax, but it remains a worthy goal. Never stop questioning. Never stop looking for ways to improve your code. I have the utmost confidence that you can take the code I've given you as a starting point and make it more robust, elegant, and bulletproof.

The Future of Ajax

9

Where Do We Go From Here?

As you write more Ajax applications, you will confront many of the same issues over and over again. Every time you solve a general problem, it'll be helpful to put that piece of JavaScript to one side so you can reuse it later. It makes sense to abstract your code into reusable pieces—that's what I did with the `Hijax` object. Eventually you will have a handy collection of code at your fingertips.

BUILDING A JAVASCRIPT LIBRARY

Here are just some of the issues that you may come across while building up your own personal library of reusable code.

Event handling

I've been using straightforward event handlers like `onclick` and `onsubmit`. These work in all browsers, but they have a major drawback: you can only assign one event to each event handler.

The W3C DOM specification provides a method called `addEventListener`. Internet Explorer doesn't support this method. Instead, Microsoft provides a proprietary method called `attachEvent`. The differences in implementations can be abstracted away by using a function like `addEvent` from John Resig (http://ejohn.org/projects/flexible-javascript-events/) or Dean Edwards (http://dean.edwards.name/weblog/2005/10/add-event2/).

Manipulating the DOM

If you aren't using `innerHTML`, generating markup takes a lot of work. You need to use a lot of DOM methods such as `createElement` and `appendChild` combined with DOM properties such as `childNodes`, `nodeName`, and so on. Instead of writing very similar code over and over, it makes sense to create reusable functions for generating markup. Dan Webb has done just that with his DOM Builder script (http://www.vivabit. com/bollocks/2006/04/06/introducing-dom-builder).

Animation

The DOM is implemented fairly consistently from browser to browser. The BOM, or Browser Object Model, is another story. Browsers use different property names for measurements such as browser width. These differences can be frustrating if you're trying to do complex animation. Again, the logical solution is to abstract away the browser differences with reusable code.

Libraries, Frameworks, and Toolkits, Oh My!

Over time, all JavaScript developers build up their own library of reusable code. Some developers have taken this a step further and released their libraries into the wild for other developers to use. These collections of functions and objects are sometimes called toolkits, or even frameworks. As far as I can tell, the terms *library, toolkit,* and *framework* are used interchangeably.

There are two reasons why you might use someone else's library:

1. Although you are well versed in DOM Scripting and Ajax, you need to save some time on a project. Rather than reinvent the wheel, you can use code that somebody else has written to solve a similar problem. You understand exactly what the code is doing and you can tweak and adjust it according to your needs.

2. Faced with a problem, you turn to a library that claims to provide a solution. The danger in using someone else's code is that you don't know how the code works, and when something goes wrong (and it will), you won't be able to fix it.

The first scenario illustrates how useful libraries are for saving time and effort. The second scenario illustrates how dangerous libraries can be for the same reasons. Using a JavaScript library is like wielding a knife: it can be a useful tool, but in the wrong hands it can cause terrible damage.

There are many JavaScript libraries out there to choose from. Let's take a look at some of the more popular options.

PROTOTYPE

Sam Stephenson of 37signals created the Prototype library (http://prototype.conio.net/). The birth of Prototype coincided with the creation of the Ruby on Rails server-side framework at the same company. The two work well together: Rails uses Prototype (and its offspring, Scriptaculous) to add JavaScript helpers. These helpers are added in an obtrusive manner, but thanks to the passionate Rails community, a patch is available (http://www.ujs4rails.com/).

The Prototype code is elegant and clean, weighing in at about 48K. Prototype is designed to make the developer's life easier by providing a number of shortcuts. For instance, instead of writing `document.getElementById("element_id")`, Prototype lets you type `$("element_id")`.

The Prototype Web site doesn't provide much documentation, but an enthusiastic fan base of bloggers is demonstrating how to use the library (http://www.prototypedoc.com/).

SCRIPTACULOUS

Prototype forms the basis of the Scriptaculous library (http://script.aculo.us/). Scriptaculous contains a series of modules that have been created with Prototype. There are separate files available for drag and drop, animation, and Ajax.

The animation module is built in a very modular way. A series of combination effects are built on top of a bundle of core effects. The Web site also provides a treasure chest of user-submitted effects.

Users provide documentation for Scriptaculous on an ongoing basis through a wiki.

MOCHIKIT

Bob Ippolito created the MochiKit library (http://mochikit.com/). Like Scriptaculous, it has been constructed in a modular fashion so that you don't have to download everything if you don't need to use all the available functionality.

The design of MochiKit is heavily influenced by the Python programming language. It is a testament to the flexibility of JavaScript that it allows itself to be adapted in this way. That said, it makes more sense to me to learn the characteristics of JavaScript rather than try to make it behave more like another language.

MochiKit provides methods such as `loadJSONDoc` and `doSimpleXMLHttpRequest` for Ajax requests. It also provides a great log function that makes debugging much easier than using a series of alert statements. All of the MochiKit methods are documented on the Web site.

JQUERY

Like Prototype, jQuery is a JavaScript library filled with shortcuts (http://jquery.com/). It even replicates the `$` function from Prototype.

The most interesting aspect of jQuery is the way it lets you chain methods together in one statement. Here is an example from the front page of the jQuery Web site:

```
$("p.surprise").addClass("ohmy").show("slow");
```

This finds all the paragraph elements that have a class of `surprise`, adds the class `ohmy` to each of them, and then slowly reveals them. This syntax is very handy for attaching multiple events and effects to elements.

jQuery is available in two versions: a compressed version (about 20K) for use in production sites and an uncompressed version (around 52K) that is more readable.

YUI

YUI is short for Yahoo User Interface library (http://developer.yahoo.com/yui/). As the name suggests, developers at Yahoo created this library. As well as talking the talk, Yahoo walks the walk: this is the same JavaScript that is used across all of Yahoo's worldwide properties.

Rather than providing one monolithic code structure, YUI is split into separate modules called utilities. There are utilities for events, animation, drag and drop, DOM manipulation, and Ajax. The Ajax utility is called the connection manager.

Unlike Prototype and jQuery, brevity is not the main goal of YUI. Priority is given instead to ensuring that the library's JavaScript plays nicely with your own code. Everything is encapsulated within an object called `YAHOO`. Here's an example of an event handler:

```
YAHOO.util.event.addListener("element_id", "click",
myFunction);
```

As well as the core utilities, YUI provides controls for common Web application widgets such as sliders, calendars, and menus.

Because YUI is in active development by a big organization, the documentation for the library is very detailed. Best of all, Yahoo developers are also documenting the research behind the utilities (http://developer.yahoo.com/ypatterns/). Called the Design Pattern Library, this offers invaluable insight into the complexities behind seemingly simple interactions such as drag and drop.

Choosing a Library

I've listed just some of the JavaScript libraries that are freely available. There are many more, such as Dojo, originally developed by Alex Russell and now maintained by the Dojo Foundation (http://dojotoolkit.org/). Mootools is another popular library (http://mootools.net/).

If you want to get a feel for any of these libraries, try downloading them and playing around with the code. When you are evaluating a library, there are a number of factors to bear in mind.

FILE SIZE

Because JavaScript is a client-side language, the end user will need to download whichever library you choose. Nobody likes long download times. You will need to decide if the waiting time is offset by the benefits provided by the library. The modular structure of some libraries allows you to pick and choose the bare minimum amount of code for your needs.

DOCUMENTATION

Documentation matters. A library might be filled with powerful features, but without a set of instructions, those features will languish unused.

Most libraries provide some kind of documentation on their Web sites. The style of documentation varies. Some libraries have very technical documentation that isn't very pleasurable to read. On the other hand, there are quite a few blog posts about the practical usage of libraries, which are generally more readable.

BROWSER SUPPORT

It is common practice at the beginning of a Web design project to specify a baseline of browsers that will be actively supported. This list of browsers should be as inclusive as possible. Likewise, every JavaScript library has its own list of supported browsers. The more cross-browser–compatible a library is, the better. Your browser baseline should not change to accommodate a fussy library. If a library does not work in all the browsers that you need to support, don't use that library.

Whither Ajax?

The abundance of JavaScript libraries seems like a boon for Web developers, but their very existence raises a troubling question. Is JavaScript—and by extension, Ajax—really so complex that we require third-party toolkits to solve our problems?

For the level of Ajax that I have covered in this book, I believe that using a library would be overkill. For more complex, animation-rich applications, a library could certainly save a lot of time and effort.

As applications grow more complex, the need for cross-browser shortcuts increases. However, as the complexity of a Web application increases, its robustness declines. It becomes increasingly difficult to employ progressive enhancement. Providing access for screen-reader users moves from being tricky to downright Sisyphean.

Given this steep difficulty curve, it makes sense to keep Ajax enhancements lightweight and subtle. Yet most Ajax applications on the Web today are quite complex.

FROM DESKTOP TO WEB BROWSER

A common yardstick for measuring the perceived success of an Ajax application is how well it mirrors the desktop experience. Web developers are attempting to emulate the experience of using native applications. The results are called Rich Internet Applications.

I am not convinced by this scramble for RIAs. The term itself implies that non-RIAs, if they aren't rich, must be poor Internet applications. There is a fallacy in assuming that a rich user interface equates to a rich user experience. In my experience, the opposite can be true. Some of the most rewarding, emotionally involving experiences I've had on the Web were on plain, text-heavy sites. Some of my most frustrating experiences involved highly interactive but unusable Web applications.

What's good for the desktop is not necessarily good for the Web browser. Drag and drop is a case in point. This convention is used in many Ajax applications but rarely with the same thought that has gone into native desktop apps. If I want to move a file from my computer's desktop to the trash, I can drag and drop it, but I can also use the keyboard or navigate using the file system. Dragging and dropping is only one way of accomplishing my task. When this convention is borrowed by Ajax applications, alternate solutions are seldom provided.

For many developers, the term *Ajax* has come to mean any kind of desktop-like interaction on the Web. For me, Ajax is fundamentally about asynchronous communication with a Web server from within a Web browser. Desktop software can teach us many lessons about interface and interaction design, but we must not lose sight of the fact that Ajax is a Web technology at heart. If you decide to borrow conventions from the desktop, make sure you don't break the fundamental expectations of interaction on the Web.

Users expect to initiate interaction by clicking on links and buttons or by filling in forms. With progressive enhancement, it is possible to ensure that these kinds of interactions degrade gracefully to hyperlinked documents and form submissions.

Ajax is pushing the boundaries of Web browsers' capabilities, which is exciting. It's important that the Web evolves and moves forward. At the same time, it's equally important that the fundamental nature of the Web remains undamaged. The World Wide Web is a wondrous collection of documents linked together through the beautifully simplistic power of hypertext. Used well, Ajax can enhance the experience of navigating and enjoying this virtual cornucopia. Used carelessly, Ajax could sever the very connections that define the Web.

THANK YOU

Thank you for reading this book. I've shown you some code, but I'm sure you can improve on what you've seen here. More importantly, I hope I've shown you how crucial it is to have a questioning attitude when it comes to Ajax. Question the way you implement Ajax. Question the impact Ajax will have on your users. Question the need to use Ajax at all.

Ajax is a cool technology, but that's not a good reason to use it. Ajax can improve usability: that's a much better reason to use it. I'm sure you will use Ajax to enhance your Web sites to be more powerful without sacrificing access to your content.

Creating bulletproof Ajax is challenging, but the rewards are worth it. Good luck.

Index

reusable code
    in Bulletproof books example, 167–176
        closures, 170–173
        completing requests, 176
        initiating requests, 173–176
        writing objects, 168–170
    JavaScript libraries and, 189–193
RGB values, 131–132
Rich Internet Applications (RIA's), 194–195
"Roadmap for Accessible Rich Internet Applications", 150
role for screen readers, 150
Ruby on Rails server-side framework, 190
Russell, Alex, 193

S

Safari
    animation and, 126
    XMLHttpRequest support and, 47
scalar data types, 20
scope of variables, 30–31
screen readers
    Ajax and, 142–145
    basics of, 141
    Bulletproof books example, 185–186
    bypassing Ajax, 147–148
    detecting, 149
    FlashAir and, 149
    future technology, 150–151
    state of the art, 146–149
    Web browsers and, 141–142
script
    defined, 15
    script element, 82–83
    script tag hack, JSON, 82–83
    <script> tag, 98, 99
    writing in XML, 72–73
Scriptaculous library, 191
searchYahoo function, 83, 84, 85
select elements, 112
semicolons (;)
    in functions, 29
    in for loops, 27
    in statements, 15

send method, 55–56
sendData function, 111, 113, 114, 129
server-side languages, 8
session variables for storing values, 160
setAttribute method, 42, 74
setContainer method, 177
setRequestHeader method, 55–56
setters, DOM, 41–43
setTimeout function, 131
setTimeout statement, 184
shopping cart functionality (Bulletproof books example), 161–162, 167
shoppingcart.php file, 161, 166
slashes (//) in JavaScript, 16
source code, downloading for chapter 8, 154
split function, JavaScript, 106
start method, 171, 172, 173, 174
state values, for screen readers, 150
statements, JavaScript, 15–16
status code, 57–59
Stenhouse, Mike, 136
Stephenson, Sam, 190
strings, 18–19
strong typing, 17
styling (Bulletproof books example), 162–166
submit event, 171
subtraction operators, 22
SuperNova, 141
surprise class, 192

T

tab order, updating, 143–144
tabindex attribute, 143
tabindex hack, 185
tabindex value, 144
test condition, in for loops, 27
text files, displaying contents of (example), 60–65
    JavaScript, 60–63
    markup, 63–65
text function, 170
text nodes, 37
textarea elements, 112
this keyword, 33, 168, 169